FRAGMENTS
OF YOUR
ANCIENT
NAME

365 Glimpses of the Divine
for Daily Meditation

FRAGMENTS
OF YOUR
ANCIENT
NAME

JOYCE RUPP

SORIN BOOKS Notre Dame, Indiana

Scripture quotations are from the *New Revised Standard Version* of the Bible, copyright © 1993 and 1989 by the Division of Christian Education of the National Council of Churches of Christ in the USA. Used by permission. All rights reserved.

"Each Soul Completes Me" is reprinted from the Penguin publication *Love Poems from God: Twelve Sacred Voices from the East and West*, Copyright © 2002, Daniel Ladinsky and used with his permission.

"Ich lese es heraus aus deinem Wort / I read it here in your very word," from *Rilke's Book of Hours: Love Poems to God* by Rainer Maria Rilke, translated by Anita Barrows and Joanna Macy, Copyright © 1996 by Anita Barrows and Joanna Macy. Used by permission of Riverhead Books, an imprint of Penguin Group (USA) Inc.

www.sorinbooks.com

ISBN-10 1-933495-28-6 ISBN-13 978-1-933495-28-6

Cover image iStockphoto.com.

Cover and text design by Katherine Robinson Coleman.

Printed and bound in the United States of America.

Library of Congress Cataloging-in-Publication Data

Rupp, Joyce.

  Fragments of your ancient name : 365 glimpses of the divine for daily meditation / Joyce Rupp.

    p. cm.

  Includes bibliographical references and indexes.

  ISBN-13: 978-1-933495-28-6

  ISBN-10: 1-933495-28-6

  1. God--Name--Meditations. 2. Devotional calendars. I. Title.

  BL473.R87 2011

  202'.11--dc22

                           2010047858

To
the One
encompassing all names
and no names
singing
in my soul
since the beginning

I read it here in your very word,
in the story of the gestures
with which your hands cupped themselves
around our becoming—limiting, warm.
You said *live* out loud, and *die* you said lightly,
and over and over again you said *be*.
But before the first death came murder.
A fracture broke across the rings you'd ripened.
A screaming shattering the voices
that had just come together to speak you,
to make of you a bridge
over the chasm of everything.
And what they have stammered ever since
are fragments
of your ancient name.

—*Rainer Maria Rilke*

Contents

Acknowledgments

A woman rarely births a child all alone. An author does not birth a book alone either. This is certainly true regarding *Fragments of Your Ancient Name*. Countless individuals have contributed directly and indirectly to what I have written. Because I journeyed with this book for about fifteen years, the names of some persons have slipped through the sleeve of time and been forgotten. However, there are many whose influence remains vividly alive to me.

There is one person I especially want to acknowledge, Mary Hogan, O.S.M. It was Mary who awakened me to the possibility of naming the divine with something besides the customary titles. Others have since also contributed options to use, particularly Pat Carson, Nancy Marsh, O.S.M., Suzie Massey, Gabriella Micallef, Maria Micallef, Pat Sircy, and Pat Sloan Skinner. My longtime friend Macrina Wiederkehr, O.S.B., not only contributed ideas for names, but she also gave her precious time to read part of the text and offered valuable suggestions.

During the past several years, I have been gifted with much-needed space, solitude, and beauty of nature to work on the manuscript. How grateful I am for the generosity and kindness of those who found either a place for me to write or offered me their own home to do so: Augusta Tapia; Billy and Patty Dorgan at Point Clear, Alabama; Chris O'Brien, O.S.M., and the Servite Friars at Benburb, Northern Ireland; Dan and Peggy Patenaude at East Falmouth, Massachussetts; Katie Bloom, Marilyn Offutt, and Rose Roeder at Lake Okoboji, Iowa; Mary Ann Gisler, O.S.B., and staff at Bethlehem Centre at Nanaimo, British Columbia; Patty Dennis and Nona Dennis at North Bay, Ontario; Thomas Little and staff at Bon Secours Spirituality Center in Mariottsville, Maryland.

My vision of how to name the divine expanded significantly due to my Sufi mentor, Irene Lazarus, and to the leadership of Timothy Dobson at the weekly Dances of Universal Peace in Boulder, Colorado.

When it came to an initial editing of the manuscript, I called on the vibrant women's spirituality group to which I belong. These dear women's critique and depth of insight about the manuscript gifted me enormously with confidence and encouragement: Shelley Erickson, Mary Ferring, Joyce Hutchison, Mary Jones, Becky Kemble, Mary Mahoney, Kathy Quinn, Kathy Reardon, and Kathi Sircy.

How blessed I am to have collaborated with Robert Hamma of Ave Maria Press. Not only did his editorial skills improve the book, he also offered unwavering support and kindness.

I would not have the focus and energy to write were it not for Faye Williamsen, my website creator and manager. Nor would I have the internal stamina and daily commitment to stay with the ups and downs of writing without the prayers of those who pray for me daily. Thank you, especially, to Colleen Erb, Janet Barnes, Bernard and Joan McLaughlin, Therese McGratty, and Frieda Molinelli.

Fragments of Your Ancient Name contains a year's worth of glimpses of the divine. As you will note in the indexes, the variety of names comes from authors, composers of music, poets, theologians, and diverse religious sources. The originators of these names unknowingly entered this book and allowed me much to ponder as I wrote the reflections based on those glimpses. To all I offer my sincere and humble gratitude.

Thank you to each person who urged me to write this book and who helped me to birth it by cheering me on. May the One who is known by many names be a source of ever-deepening peace and happiness for you.

Introduction

There are never enough names and images
for what we love.

—Dorothee Soelle

No one knows for certain who voiced the first name
for divinity or when this happened. At some point
in history a stirring in the human spirit led to this significant moment. Did this take place when a man or woman
felt a curious desire to name an unexplained inner presence? Perhaps it was during a quiet time as they contem-
plated the recurrent changing of seasons or after a person
died a tragic death and questions arose about the afterlife.
Did it occur when the marvel of fire was birthed or when
one of them stood in silent awe before the ebb and flow
of the sea? Could it have been when male and female
became aware of how they created another of their own
kind through sexual union? We can only imagine what
the movement in the human spirit was like when someone sensed this mysterious presence and tried to create
a name for the divine. How intriguing and perplexing it
must have been.

The countless titles given to divinity from earliest
times down to the present era reflect humanity's attempt
to communicate with this veiled presence. This desire
to relate to divinity can be found in the ancient names
of gods and goddesses who were believed to express

1

particular energies of the deity. We do have historical documents, theological explanations, and religious scriptures indicating how individuals and societies throughout the ages have sought to connect with the numinous One. These sources tell how humankind followed intuitions arising from moments of mystery, wonderment at the natural world, human intimacy and unexplained experiences of body, mind, and spirit.

In spite of the sources describing and defining divinity, the hunt is still on today for further aspects of this hidden presence. Women and men continue to create ways to address and describe this Indescribable One. They still elicit names that correspond to current cultural ideas and personal experiences of this sublime deity. Yet, they glean only glimpses of this mystery.

Why, after all these years, have we been unable to completely wrap our minds and hearts around words describing this sought-after-One? Could it be that humankind did not need to do this in the beginning? Perhaps the human race was so fully united with divinity that words were unnecessary. The German poet Rainier Maria Rilke offers this notion as a possibility. In the poem opening this book, he presents a tender image of the warm hands of the author of life cupped "around our becoming." It is an image of eternal goodness embracing created life. Rilke imagines this as a time in which the cycle of life and death moves within a natural, comfortable pattern:

> You said *live* out loud, and *die* you said lightly,
> and over and over again you said *be*.

Within this natural rhythm humanity "had just come together." Men and women were able to communicate with the divine, to be at home with this oneness ("a bridge/ over the chasm of everything"). But then violence erupted from within the human spirit and harshly upset the natural rhythm of life and death. Human aggression flared forth and fractured the peaceful cycle. At the very moment when the pattern of their lives flowed smoothly, they rejected it through the deliberate breakage of human relationship.

Rilke refers to this violence between humans as a "shattering." This fracturing made it difficult for them to know and name the divine being. The poet depicts humankind's attempt to communicate with divinity after this self-imposed division as a stammering:

> And what they have stammered ever since
> are fragments
> of your ancient name.

Since that time, Rilke tells us, all names and descriptions for the deity are only small clues to knowing this secreted love. The contradictory nature of human beings keeps the search and longing for complete union incomplete. Although men and women try to piece together the seamless essence of divinity, they end up with infinitesimal parts of the exquisite wholeness. The names that humans provide to portray this sacred essence contain only a hint of the one who stirs within the heart and life of each created being.

Thus it is within the brokenness of our humanity that we speak of the Holy One. Each glimpse allows us a step further on the bridge uniting us with this eternal goodness.

Each name enhances our relationship with the One who exists as the underpinning of our love.

NAMING DIVINITY

The naming of divinity within certain religions evokes a profound solemnity. Some faiths will not voice the entirety of the Divine One's name due to reverence. Christians profess their belief in the power of the divine name by ending their prayers with "We ask this in the name of Jesus" (Jn 16:23) They are encouraged to "bend the knee at the name of Jesus" (Phil 2:11) and to "gather in his name" (Mt 18:20). In their universal prayer, the Our Father, Christians pray "hallowed be thy name" (Lk 11:2).

Within the Jewish scriptures when Moses asks who is sending him, he receives this response: "You shall say to the Israelites, *I AM* has sent me to you" (Ex 13–14). Moses is also the one who receives the Ten Commandments, which includes the mandate "You shall not make wrongful use of the name of the Lord your God, for the Lord will not acquit anyone who misuses his name" (Ex 20:7).

Individuals throughout the Bible are given names that often indicate certain characteristics and qualities of significance. Oftentimes these are bestowed on people after an encounter with divinity. Among the numerous renamings is Sarai ("my princess") who receives the new designation of Sarah ("mother of nations") after her son is born in her old age (Gn 17:15). She names him Isaac, meaning "laughter," because "God has brought laughter for me; everyone who hears will laugh with me" (Gn 21:6). An angel tells Hagar to call her child Ishmael, meaning "God hears," because "the Lord has given heed to your affliction" (Gn 16:11). Saul's name is changed to Paul after his conversion to emphasize his new identity (Acts 9:1–30; 13:9).

As individuals are named, so is the Holy One whom they honor. Modern society is accustomed to speaking about and addressing divinity with the word "God," a title directly rooted in the word "good." When *U.S. Catholic* magazine interviewed religious historian Karen Armstrong, she responded in this way to a question about the notion of "God":

> In his *Summa Theologica*, [Thomas] Aquinas starts out by saying we cannot define God. Then he gives five ways, as he calls them, to think about God, all variations of the fact that nothing can come out of nothing: the intelligent designer, the first cause that must have started the universe, and so forth. He ends each by saying this is what everybody means when they say "God." Then he immediately pulls the rug out from under our feet, saying that we have no idea what such a being is or how it can exist. We can't even say it exists. All we've proved is the existence of a mystery.

It is this same Thomas Aquinas that Elizabeth Johnson quotes in *Quest for the Living God* as she emphasizes our need to expand our views of divinity: "We see the necessity of giving to God many names." Edward Hays writes in his creative *Prayers for a Planetary Pilgrim* of the expansiveness and mystery of "God": "You elude all names we give you and dwell beyond the grasp of brilliant minds."

Trappist monk Thomas Merton, more than any other, has been my spiritual mentor. It is particularly from his writings that I have gained encouragement and affirmation of my own experience of naming and relating to "God." Merton's writings affirm my belief that I can communicate with this divine entity. In *New Seeds of Contemplation* Merton explains:

> There is no "what" that can be called God. There is "no such thing" as God because God is neither a "what," nor a "thing," but a pure "*Who*" . . . the "Thou" before whom our inmost "I" springs into awareness . . . the I Am before whom with our own most personal and inalienable voice we echo "I am."

This ability to commune with the Divine One sustained the brave Jewish woman, Etty Hillisum, who died at the hands of the Nazis in Auschwitz at the age of twenty-nine. In *An Interrupted Life*, she writes in one of her journal entries, "I repose in myself. And that part of myself, that deepest and richest part in which I repose, is what I call 'God'." This deep, rich part of our inner being is the nucleus of Merton's relationship with the Holy One. "God" most certainly remains full of mystery but is equally knowable through the daily revelations of goodness that we experience. Merton refers to this specifically in *Zen and the Birds of Appetite*, where he notes that "the personal God" is "the *deepest center* of consciousness and unification." He then goes on to explain that we develop this relationship "by the active and creative awareness of love, which is our highest good."

This is where naming the divinity can take us, to a deeper union with the divine, to a fuller knowing and expression of love in our lives. "God" is not an object, but a reachable, experienced presence. At the same time, "God" is not an essence to be grasped or squeezed into my small space of intelligence. Vast and mysterious. Up close and personal. Both of these dimensions manifest in my perception of "God."

When I first started writing reflections on the names, I did not intend this book to contain prayers. I began by giving explanations and descriptions of each one. After writing about a dozen of these, I found myself addressing the Divine One directly. What I quickly re-learned is that when we "name," we connect. A personal dimension evolves. Naming allows for relationship. Each designation or title I held in my heart drew me *into* the relationship *with* "God" rather than keeping me outside as an objective observer. When we name anyone or anything, there's the possibility of coming closer. In the case of naming divinity, this can have an influence on how we relate to this presence and on the way we live.

In *New Seeds of Contemplation,* Thomas Merton writes that our idea of divinity tells us more about ourselves than it does about the divine. The names we use are personal projections of our own humanness and our perceptions about life. Because of our inability to adequately perceive who this Nameless One is, we tend to project or place on "God" our beliefs, inclinations, and hopes about divinity.

In our efforts to describe and connect with the Divine One, we thus attribute human-like characteristics and qualities in order to explain who and what this sacred essence is. We cannot literally picture divinity, so we speak of this beloved one through analogy, using metaphor, symbol, story, and words of our making (God, my rock . . . my fortress . . . my resting place). The titles we give to divinity reflect our varied life experiences whether these be ones of jubilation and celebration or sorrow and defeat. Every part of life holds possibilities of analogy for naming "God."

When I reflected on the names in this book, I noticed how my personality, life experience, religious beliefs, and personal spirituality flavored the lines I penned, particularly those that have their roots in my own faith. As a Christian formed by the teachings of Jesus of Nazareth, I am influenced by the belief that Jesus revealed the divine qualities through his life. Knowing this, I tried to connect with the teachings and spirituality of other religious traditions, as well. I researched how different religions and scholars interpret and explain names such as the Jewish "Shekinah," the Chinese "Kuan Yin," and the Native American "Wakan-Tanka."

Because our concepts of divinity flow from analogies, our glimpses or names for the divine reflect countless paradoxes. They also allow for a nondualistic approach: the Divine One is hidden but also revealed, changing and unchanging, unconditionally loving but also judging, maker of light but also maker of darkness, transcendent yet immanent, and so forth. The gift of images and symbols is that they contain many layers and nuances. For example, when "Light" refers to the Divine One, this symbol might connote an aspect such as the clear radiance of revelation, or a bright ray of guidance, a beam of truth, or a glow that comforts.

Although we endow "God" with attributes of our imagination, there is only one ultimate reality into which all these traits dissolve. Renowned religious historian Huston Smith commented in *Gnosis* magazine about "the God beyond qualities" and pointed out that when we move beyond the personal attributes we give to the divine "all the attributes of the personal God melt down into an ultimate unity that we cannot imagine, though it is actually the only *true* reality." Like the parable of the blind persons trying to describe what an elephant is as each one holds on to a different part of the animal, the same with divinity. Each name is just a glimpse of the mysterious "*I Am.*"

The knowledge that our names for divinity consists of projections and that our perception of the Divine One is limited could be a source of frustration and doubt. Or it could lead to more exploration and wonderment. My response has been an eager interest in further exploration. I am enthralled with never being able to fully comprehend the totality of divinity. There is always another aspect to be discovered that might confirm or add to my understanding and experience of the One who has captured my heart.

EXPANDING OUR NOTION OF WHO "GOD" IS

Long ago I was startled by a comment of theologian Sandra Schneiders: "God is more than two men and a bird." I laughed, but then realized her challenge to go beyond the names I had for the Blessed Trinity or the Roman Catholic sign of the cross. Soon after this I heard a sister in my community begin an opening prayer with "God of the Morning." I recall feeling slightly amazed. I never would have thought to use this name. On that day I woke up to the adventure of expanding how I view and address the divine.

Until then my vision of the Holy One was extremely limited. When J. B. Phillips wrote the following in *Your God Is Too Small*, he could have been writing it directly to me:

The trouble with many people today is that they have
not found a God big enough for modern needs. While
their experience of life has grown in a score of directions,
and their mental horizons have been expanded to the
point of bewilderment by world events and by scientific
discoveries, their ideas of God have remained largely
static.

He then goes on to give some examples of "unreal Gods"
such as Resident Policeman, Absolute Perfection, Managing Director, and Grand Old Man.

Names for divinity often evolve from the cultural and
spiritual atmosphere of the times. "The Litany of the Sacred
Heart" is an example. This long list of aspects related to
Jesus' life and love was approved in 1899 by Pope Leo XIII,
many centuries after Jesus lived. We can see this evolution
of names being influenced by current scientific theories in
titles such as the "the Cosmic Christ."

Society continues to explore possibilities for naming
divinity. In Alice Walker's novel, *The Color Purple*, Shug
says, "God ain't a he or a she, but a It." In *The Shack*, author
William Paul Young presents the Trinity as an African
American woman, a Middle Eastern man with a large nose,
and a delicate Asian girl. These images sometimes shock
and offend. But they can serve to unlatch a closed mind that
keeps the divine stuffed in a small box, expecting everyone
else to do the same.

"God" is much more than our human minds and hearts
know and experience. Yet, something in us wants surety,
finality, absoluteness. Too often the Divine One has become
a god over whom people fight. In another poem from *Love
Poems to God*, Rilke warns of a tendency to restrict the divine

to our own images and gestures until they stand around us "like a thousand walls." His words remind me that the chosen names we have for the divine will limit us if we decide they are the only ones worthy of allowing us, or anyone else, to communicate with disguised divinity. These names then get fenced-in and become barriers, rather than bridges, to the Holy One.

I learned to not be afraid that the names used by other religions might take away from my own relationship and understanding of who the divine is. This was my initial fear, but I gradually realized that a mixture of names can provide an enlarged awareness of religious diversity and a stronger love for divinity. What tears us apart is a sense of superiority and a hostile rejection of those whose religious traditions are other than our own. Wars are fought, people killed, nature destroyed, families divided, theologians and writers silenced by church authorities, all by those self-righteously claiming that "my God is better than your God."

This defensive posturing (and sometimes outright hatred) often stems from misconceptions and ignorance regarding other religions and their naming of divinity. This was the situation in a negative message I received from a woman telling me that she and her prayer group had ceased using one of my books because I included a page with a Muslim name for the divine. She wrote how offended she felt "because the Word of God states that we should not worship any other gods." What she did not realize, of course, is that Muslims, Jews, and Christians all profess belief in the one divine being.

It is not my intent with these many names to suggest that all religions are basically the same. They are not. No one has to accept another's ideas or expressions of the divine, but each one needs to respect another's beliefs. Even if another's naming of divinity does not stem from the Abrahamic sources, respect is due. Each person's approach arises from a desire to connect in some way with this ineffable presence of love. If we can open our minds and hearts, we may well find that the varied attributes of divinity expand our vision of who "God" is and draw us deeper into relationship with this Holy One.

I've come to accept wholeheartedly what Miriam Therese Winter writes in *Paradoxology*:

> God-images change as times change, and even as we change. Christianity has outgrown that familiar God-image of an aging patriarch presiding over heaven and keeping tabs on Earth. In this age of cosmological awareness, we now acknowledge and gratefully celebrate the cosmos as the embodiment of God. . . . The images and names I have for God are markers on my spiritual journey that reflect a theological evolution through layer after layer of an inner unfolding, preparing the way for cosmic wisdom in a quantum universe.

The biggest challenge for me in naming the divine was incorporating a feminine dimension. In 1978, Pope John Paul I said, "We need to call God 'mother' as well as 'father'." Ten years passed after that before I developed a personal relationship with divinity that included truly being at home with "Mother, Sister, Sophia," and other feminine designations. Today I cannot imagine attributes of divinity without including these feminine names. They balance the overabundance of masculine characteristics projected onto the Divine One and contain qualities that are essential to a holistic relationship with divinity.

I prefer to think of names for divinity not as definitions but as *expansions*, as a broadening of our understanding and experience of this magnificent mystery. Rabbi Rami Shapiro alludes to this in his monthly *Spirituality and Health* column:

> God cannot be named. Aware of the suffering caused by gods created in our own image for our own profit, I vow to recognize all ideas about God as products of human beings, bound by history and circumstance, and forever incapable of defining the Reality Beyond Naming.

DISCOVERING AND GATHERING THE NAMES

No matter how well we plan our lives, unexpected events enter to change us in profound and surprising ways. Such was the case fifteen years ago when I moved to Boulder, Colorado, for graduate studies at Naropa University. It was during those two years that I became acquainted with Sufism, something foreign to me and which I had no intention of discovering or exploring. While living in Boulder I trained to work as a hospice volunteer. In doing so, I met a Sufi who introduced me to the "Ninety-Nine Most Beautiful Names," the descriptive titles for Allah. Most of these are derived from Islam's holy scripture, the Qur'an. The Sufis, a mystical branch of Islam, chant these names in a spiritual practice known as *zikr* or *dkihr*. The purpose of a lengthy repetition of one or more of the names is not only to remember and honor the divine, but to also create spiritual transformation in the heart of the chanter.

At the first *zikr* I attended, I was immediately drawn into the power of singing one of the "most beautiful names." Accessing the variety of names in Sufism lifted my spirit and drew me deeper into union with the One who has been a part of my life since early childhood. Memories arose from my Roman Catholic heritage of reciting various litanies. The chanting also reminded me of the Taizé chants, lovely Christian repetitions created in modern times by the French community.

Years after my experiences with *zikr* in Boulder, I returned to spend a weekend with another tradition of chanting names for the divine: the ancient Hindu practice of *kirtan,* which consists of antiphonally singing devotional hymns in which devotees alternate with a leader. Again, I found myself drawn to unite with the Source of Love and to activate this love in my life.

All this is to say that I've been drawn into exploring the variety of attributes given to divinity for quite some time. More than ten years ago, I started a file and began gathering names. I first combed the scriptures of the three Abrahamic religions of Judaism, Christianity, and Islam. While these three religions all profess belief in one divine being, each gives this being a different, basic name: Yahweh, God, and Allah. I discovered that besides the Ninety-Nine Most Beautiful Names of the Sufi tradition (whose listing of names varies), there is an encyclopedia of names in the Jewish mystical tradition, and in the early Syrian Christian community there were at least one hundred names for Jesus.

As the years sped by, I found names for the divine in songs, poems, prayers, theological writings and spirituality books, novels and other literature. Friends and acquaintances also slipped suggestions to me. In this book I have listed the origin of the names next to each one, but the name may well be found in another source, too. Some titles have no reference because I either created them myself or discovered them through some unknown or forgotten source. No doubt I have missed a few significant ones. Some names I omitted due to duplication of the quality attributed to the divine. Others, such as the foundational one of "love," found their way into a variety of reflections.

MY HOPE FOR THE READER

When I first began writing this book, I felt confident that I would find a name for each day of the year. This did, indeed, happen. Up to the time of closing work on my manuscript I was still uncovering more names. As I penned the first few reflections, I wondered, however, if I would get to a hundred fifty and be unable to go on. To my happy surprise I never once halted in the process. Each day another aspect tumbled forth into words, another glimpse flowed into print. Even now I am amazed that this occurred. I am left with profound gratitude for the movement of Love's inspiration.

I encourage you to contemplate the names. Be full of curiosity. Engage each one with the wonder of an open mind and heart. Let the reflections deepen an appreciation in you for the divine. Let them stretch you into a fuller, more expansive view of this mysterious one. Hold dear the name of the One you cherish, but also lend your heart to the ones that are uncomfortable or unusual. Call on the divine as you go about your life using the name given for that particular day.

My expectation is that *Fragments of Your Ancient Name* will expand your sense of who divinity might be and allow for some movement beyond safe boundaries. I hope these reflections strengthen your faith by contributing to a vibrant relationship with the divine and that they increase your respect for those who see "God" differently than you do. Through reflecting on these names, may you find whatever it is you most need to be a person of great love.

It is to Rainier Maria Rilke's *Love Poems to God* I once more turn as a final thought about who the divine might be:

> You are the deep innerness of all things,
> the last word that can never be spoken.
> To each of us you reveal yourself differently:
> to the ship as a coastline, to the shore as a ship.

January

My soul finds its place in the Name, and my soul finds its ease in the embrace of the Name. I struggled with shapes and with numbers, and I carved with blade and brain to make a place, but I could not find a shelter for my soul. Blessed is the Name which is the safety of the soul . . . and the health of the innermost breath. I search the words that attend your mercy. You lift me out of destruction, and you win my soul. You gather it out of the unreal by the power of your name. Blessed is the Name that unifies demand, and changes the seeking into praise. Out of the panic, out of the useless plan, I awaken to your name, and solitude to solitude all your creatures speak, and through the inaccessible intention all things fall gracefully. Blessed is the shelter of my soul, blessed is the form of mercy, blessed is the Name.

—*Leonard Cohen*

I Am That I Am

Exodus 3:14

I bow before you who have no name.
Your intimate presence startles my soul
Like the first glimpse of a rising moon.
Your unwavering, companioning love
Flows like a golden rivulet of kindness
Through the veins of my truest self.
Born out of my desire to communicate
I ask for the simplest of gifts from you,
The privilege to call you by many names,
The blessing of communicating with you.

Today: I think about my favorite name for the divine.

———————————————┼———————————————

Namer of the Stars

Psalm 147:3–4

Looking up into the glittering galaxies
I see a breathtaking canopy of light.
Each twinkle leads to another and another,
Stretching out into an endless universe.
Every star reveals an immensity of mystery
And stirs in the soul a connection with you.
You touch the heavens with sparkling beauty
As you call each bright luminary into its place.
Namer of the Stars, Creator of Wonder,
I bow to the eternal brightness that is you.

Today: The *Namer of Stars* leads me to wonder.

Absolute Mystery

Karl Rahner

No amount of endless rationalizing,
No incessant stewing of the exploring mind,
No pressured tactics of spiritual dissection,
None of this will reveal your secluded depths.
Only when the hunting soul comes near you
With respectful openness and humble desire,
Will the immensity of your simple presence
Shine forth with strobe-light awareness.
Only then can one fully respond, "I believe"
And rest in a laser beam of confident faith.

Today: I rest quietly with *Absolute Mystery*.

JANUARY 4

Ancient Love

Carolyn McDade

When did the first whisper of your primeval love
Touch with infinite tenderness all that exists?
When did your kiss awaken each sleeping atom?
When did you breathe life into every particle?
Oh, Ancient Love, forever gliding through the ages,
You continually birth yourself into creation
Including this present moment of flowing life.
You whisper in this day with similar tenderness,
Reverberating in the beating heart of existence.
You are a steady cadence of love within us all.

Today: I rejoice at *Ancient Love* dancing in life.

$+$

Dreamer

O Dreamer who quietly enters my life
With your basketful of transforming symbols,
You come sailing the inaudible night skies
Within the silent corridors of my sleep,
Bringing the needed truths I rarely perceive
In the bold, glaring light of my active days.
Hearken to me with your messengers.
Gift me, please, with dreams of revelation
So the uncertain path I trod to my true self
Becomes ever clearer and ready to walk.

Today: I await with confidence the *Dreamer's* revelations.

JANUARY 6

━━━━━━━━━━━━━━━╋━━━━━━━━━━━━━━━

All-Seeing One

Job 28:23–24

I look as far as I can into future days, weeks, months,
Desiring to see what is ahead and waiting for me.
But my vision is limited and clouded with desire.
I return to seeing only what is in this present moment.
I do not need to know that which is far beyond.
I have only to trust you to direct me, All-Seeing One.
The gradual disclosure of what is best for my life
Will reveal itself when the appropriate time comes.
It is enough for me to rely on your endless affection
And to listen carefully to your wisdom within me.

Today: I trust the presence of the *All-Seeing One*.

Jesus

Matthew 1:21

Jesus, your name has been on my lips
Since I was a young and innocent child.
Now these many years since first we met
I understand you are more than a name.
To know you is to allow your teachings
To reach into the core of my daily life,
To have your vision be the vital substance
Of what truly guides and rules how I live.
How easy to bend the knee to your name
But how difficult it is to bend the heart.

Today: I make an effort to love as *Jesus* did.

Guiding Star

Matthew 2:1–2

Like the wise ones who sought the Christ Child,
I have trekked for eons in the aimless dark
Moving by faith within my inner landscapes
Without a detailed map, and full of questions.
In spite of all that seems void and doubtful,
My seeking of you has never been halted.
When the searching path to you grows faint
You appear as my trusted Guiding Star,
A beacon of hope beckoning me onward,
Manifesting your presence in surprising ways.

Today: I walk by the *Guiding Star* of faith.

Joy of Every Loving Heart

Charles Wesley

Y̶ou are the gift unable to be kept secret,
Leaping out from the happiness of sharing.
You are the blessing of intentional kindness,
The sigh of satisfaction in generous giving.
You are the reward of helping hands,
The natural euphoria of each caring heart.
You are the quiet bliss of assured contentment
Coming forth from hospitable gestures.
You are the look of love in hearts that receive,
The quiet pleasure in gracious acceptance.

Today: I find *Joy* in both giving and receiving.

———————————————┼———————————————

Allah

The Qur'an

Your name, Allah, is voiced reverently on Muslim lips.
You are their "most merciful and compassionate."
Allah, your title is rarely used by Christians and Jews,
Yet , we are joined, we three, in a common heritage.
Abraham and Sarah, they are ancestors of us all.
In each of the three religions you are the same true One.
Why this awkwardness in addressing you as Allah?
Where does my resistant, biased hesitation originate?
Help me break through, to go beyond my comfort zone,
To choose to freely speak your treasured name in Islam.

Today: *Allah* is on my lips and in my heart.

Abba

Mark 14:36

Abba, father, kind parent, gentle daddy.
Strength balanced with a caring concern.
A trusted lap in the early years of childhood.
An inner, assuring voice to be counted on.
Guiding hand of love held forth for confidence.
The deliberate stance of ready protection.
No wonder Jesus chose to call you Abba
Knowing he could lean on you for stamina.
He needed you every step of the way.
And so do I.

Today: I lean on the strength of *Abba*.

Everlasting Life

John 10:28

There is nothing temporary about you.
Nothing shallow about the endless depths
Of your being. Nothing brief about the extent
Of your longevity. You are. You will be.
Always and forever. For us, with us, among us.
Constant. Sustaining. Enduring. Unending.
And you promise to each one a life
Forever united with the richness of yours.
How could we ask for anything more?
Why would we want anything less?

Today: *Everlasting Life* offers hope.

Lantern of Love

Robert Morneau

In the unclouded cottage of my soul
A watchful light remains ever vigilant.
In the thick forest of my darkest hours
There gleams a trustworthy sentinel.
In the most lost experience of searching
A beam of direction calmly lights the way.
In the painful moments of impermanence
A signal of presence softens the loneliness.
In the bleakness of disturbing trials
You, Lantern of Love, shine steadfastly.

Today: The *Lantern of Love* lights my way.

Mother

Julian of Norwich

How wide is your womb of extensive love.
How full your breasts of inner nurturance.
How caressing the vast arms of your caring.
How precious your storehouse of wisdom.
Mother, you clothe us with needed courage.
You protectively shield our self from harm,
Drawing us near to you when we are afraid.
You never doubt our merit and worth,
Even when we are doubting it ourselves.
You are the welcome we'll always receive.

Today: I am held in the arms of *Mother*.

You Who Live Next Door

Rainer Maria Rilke

I have my old ways of keeping you
From getting too close, from maybe
Requiring too much from me.
You can be my casual neighbor
Whom I occasionally stop to visit,
The one I greet in coming or going
But not my intimate companion,
Not in my household or in my bed.
I keep my distance, lest too much
Of my hidden self tumbles out.

Today: *You Who Live Next Door* invites me in.

———————————+———————————

Perpetual Becoming

Jean Markale

Like a whirling dervish your love evolves,
Twirling with wonder among the cosmic void.
At the same time you encompass each soul.
Your presence expands both far and near,
Continuous motion and uninterrupted stillness
Conveying a seeming dichotomy of your being.
The fullness of your essential nature grows,
Ever enlarging as the universe stretches out.
Oh, the boundlessness of your dynamic love!
Oh, the astonishing, unlimited expansion of you!

Today: *Perpetual Becoming* expands in me.

Sun of Justice

Latin Hymn

Sun of Justice, source of powerful energy,
Vastly more potent than the burning sun
Transforming millions of tons of hydrogen
Into helium every second of every day.
Sear our minds with the painful reality
Of those who need your protective strength.
Radiate our hearts with true concern for them.
Burn away the dross of empty indifference.
Energize us into taking deliberate action
To aid those suffering from the power of others.

Today: I join the *Sun of Justice* and act justly.

The Opener

The Qur'an

O Divine Opener, you who free us,
There are guarded, closed-tight places
Within the deeper dimensions of self,
Places that require your assistance
So our true goodness can be liberated.
Pry apart the teeth of our stubbornness.
Swing back the door of unforgiveness.
Lift up the lid on ego-centeredness.
Knock down the walls of falseness and greed
And all that prevents oneness with you.

Today: I visit one of my places of unfreedom.

Creator of Wintry Ice and Snow

Edward Hays

The untamed winds of frosted winter
Cough their way into penetrating coldness.
Heavy snowflakes swirl wildly everywhere.
You invite us to witness this fresh beauty,
To lessen complaint about its inconvenience.
You speak to grumbling hearts in this season:
"Celebrate the wonder of what is before you.
Abandon your schedules and organized plans.
Settle into the long wintry evenings of quiet
And sip the good red wine of my contentment."

Today: I accept what inconveniences me.

✝

Joyful Journeyer

When faith takes on a form and a shape,
When duty turns into welcome responsibility,
When love accepts both ease and struggle,
When prayer includes a heart of acceptance,
When living results in more giving than getting,
When silence serves as a source of listening,
When dying no longer frightens or dismays,
When emptiness leads to paradoxical fullness,
Then we know how it is to engage with you
As the Joyful Journeyer on our road of life.

Today: The *Joyful Journeyer* influences my attitude and actions.

Sophia

Proverbs 8:1

Sophia, whose name in Greek means "wisdom,"
You provide a welcome, refreshing respite
For those seeking a feminine view of divinity.
Yet, some seekers shun and even condemn you.
Others think your beautiful name is a sham.
How could a personage so enticingly alive
Be the cause for disturbing, cataclysmic concern?
Your wisdom is truly our spiritual wealth.
Your dynamic presence offers the purest guidance.
Thank you, Sophia, for the gifts you contain.

Today: I call on *Sophia* to guide me in her ways.

Revealer of Secrets

Isaiah 45:3

Secrets from the storeroom of the divine,
Disclosures as yet unnamed and restricted,
Veiled concealments awaiting revelation,
All this rests within your enormous treasury.
What could you be keeping hidden from me?
What is disguised that can enhance my growth?
How and when will you reveal something more?
All these questions rise and fall from my mind
While you, Revealer of Secrets, simply smile,
Knowing full well no one hurries this process.

Today: I open my spirit for further revelation.

✝

Calm Sea of Peace

On occasion, I am a ship in stormy waters,
Tossed about by troubling thoughts,
Rocked harshly with emotional waves.
I am a ship searching for a calmer voyage
On the smooth surface of eventual surrender.
Protect me on the rough and roiling breakers
Of difficulties that agitate and fling me around.
Calm the patterns of distressful undulation
Tossing me to and fro in life's unwanted events.
Sail my ship on the calm sea of your peace.

Today: My ship finds the *Calm Sea of Peace.*

JANUARY 24

Laughing One

What serious theologian left out your smile
When religious doctrines were being penned?
If you join us in our terrible tribulations,
Most surely you join us in our laughter, too.
Chuckling at our humorous adventures,
Taking delight in a happy child's silliness,
Enjoying our little giggles and large guffaws,
Laughing with us at the ludicrous in life.
O divine being with a sense of humor,
How could we not be aware of you?

Today: Divine laughter echoes inside of mine.

Lawgiver

Exodus 20:2–17

How well you know the human heart
With its desires, demands, and deafness.
How much you hope for each person
To bring forth what is best and not worst
As we travel this journey back home to you.
Your laws are few and born out of love.
They keep us from harming self and others
And protect us from damaging our world.
Your laws ought not to suppress and stifle
But, rather, to liberate for what is of value.

Today: I reflect on a divine law that I dislike.

Singer in My Soul

Psalm 40:3

How resonant your presence, Singer in My Soul,
As your eloquent melodies resound in my spirit.
Each song of yours brings a message, a blessing.
The breath of your love moves through the lyrics
Captivating and enticing me away from distraction.
You are attuned to every disposition and incident.
Some days you sing loudly to awaken awareness.
At other times, you sing softly to soothe and comfort.
Whatever the cadence, the style, the libretto,
Every song of yours vibrates with unwavering love.

Today: I hear the *Singer in My Soul.*

Word of Freedom

Bernadette Farrell

Word of Freedom, spoken to the imprisoned,
You support those caught in chained addictions
As they strive to release what binds them tightly.
You encourage those in abusive relationships
To stand up strongly, to reclaim their self-respect.
You cheer on those working to change systems
That oppress the vulnerable and impoverished.
You challenge those exiled from their integrity
By the allurement of falseness and entitlement.
Word of Freedom, you call to all who are enslaved.

Today: I look to see what imprisons me.

Shelter

Psalm 61:2–4

We are often like little wintered creatures
Yearning for comfort amid the wild winds,
Seeking some protection from the bitter cold
In the frosty caves of what brings us pain.
You swathe us with maternal tenderness,
A vast blanket of love spread wide enough
To enfold every part of life; a prayer shawl,
A tender coverlet comforting and protecting.
Today, stretch forth your abiding shelter.
Wrap the warmth of your safe haven around us.

Today: *Divine Shelter* covers me with kindness.

Nourisher

Luke 1:53

Through the ages you nourish hungry souls
And those who do not recognize their need
To be fed from the provisions of your grace.
Each day you supply nurture and sustenance,
Daily bounty to strengthen our endless efforts
At maintaining and improving relationships.
You give us abundant amounts of soul-food,
Continual replenishment of our spiritual stock,
More than enough to inspire us toward self-giving,
Plenty to fortify our faith and boost our hope.

Today: I notice how the *Nourisher* feeds me.

---✚---

Holy One

Isaiah 6:1–3

Holy One, how distant some have placed you,
Apart and out of reach from our ordinariness.
Yet, your presence breathes life into creation,
Brings to birth the most common of things.
You are the Holy One, familiar with earthiness.
Your touch of life-giving, creative artistry
Assigns the sacred to every facet of existence.
You gaze upon what composes each particle
And choose to call it *good.* Bow to you, I will.
But set you at a distance? That I refuse to do.

Today: I find the *Holy One* in the ordinary.

Wise and Faithful Guide

Wisdom 9:11

Each footstep on the vacillating path of life,
Each heartbeat on the rugged road of growth,
Each passage on the shifting river of renewal,
Each thoroughfare of increasing self-knowledge,
Each route on the way toward further freedom,
Requires the attendance of your wise presence.
Whether the journey is deliberate or unexpected,
Whether the voyage is taken inward or outward,
With every inch of the tentative way that I travel
I count on your companionship and teaching.

Today: I turn to my *Wise and Faithful Guide*.

February

The letters of the Name of God in Hebrew are *yod, hay, vav,* and *hay.* They are frequently mispronounced as "Yahveh." But in truth they are unutterable. Not because of the holiness they evoke, but because they are all vowels and you cannot pronounce all the vowels at once without risking respiratory injury.

This word is the sound of breathing. The holiest Name in the world, the Name of the Creator, is the sound of your own breathing.

That these letters are unpronounceable is no accident. Just as it is no accident that they are also the root letters of the Hebrew verb "to be." Scholars have suggested that a reasonable translation of the four-letter Name of God might be: The One Who Brings Into Being All That Is. So God's Name is the Name of Being itself.

—*Lawrence Kushner*

FEBRUARY 1

+

Beckoner

Song of Songs 2:8–12

You tap at the window of my heart.
You knock at the door of my busyness.
You call out in my night dreams.
You whisper in my haphazard prayer.
You beckon. You invite. You entice.
You woo. You holler. You insist:
"Come! Come into my waiting embrace.
Rest your turmoil in my easy silence.
Put aside your heavy bag of burdens.
Accept the simple peace I offer you."

Today: I hear and respond to the One who beckons.

Spiritual Power

Jane Goodall

You flow through my endeavors
With the strength of a persistent river,
Activating all I am and all I do.
How different my approach to life is
When I lose my awareness of you,
My life's most underlying influence.
When I ignore your motivating energy
I slog along on the frail course of my ego,
Casting a discontented and tired eye
On every particle that claims my attention.

Today: I am aware of *Spiritual Power* in me.

---+---

Captain of My Heart

Rabia al-Adawiyya

Do I consent to your being in charge,
Leading the daily dealings of my heart?
Am I able to yield my comfortable control
Even if I prefer to do things my own way?
Can I surrender to what I know is right
When I hear your voice within my conscience?
How do I bend my strong independence
And move in directions of your wise choosing?
O Captain of My Heart, slowly I am accepting
The wisdom of your divine authority within me.

Today: The *Captain of My Heart* is in command.

FEBRUARY 4

+

Deepest Good

When I sort through the layered texture
Of what clutters and claims my spirit,
I find you, Deepest Good, in residence.
You shine like a piece of gold inside of me.
In that tranquil, secluded district of soul
I discover my true, unblemished nature.
Teach me that there is much more to me
Than just my struggle and my failure.
Absorb me in the jewel of your love
Until I am fully one with your goodness.

Today: *Deepest Good* affects how I view myself.

Unconditional Love

You are Love like no other.
Love so large you contain our smallness.
Love so deep you accept our shallowness.
Love so strong you carry our weakness.
Love so wide you enclose our wandering.
Love so tender you experience our hurting.
Love so tolerable you outlive our apathy.
Love so ardent you thaw our coldness.
Love so true you endure our betrayals.
Love so patient you wait for our returning.

Today: I accept that I am loved unconditionally.

Friend

John 15:15

Where would I be without you
As my confidante and companion?
How would I navigate life's troubles
Without you there to advise me?
Your faithful friendship provides
Vitality, encouragement, confidence,
And endless ingredients of joy.
I learn from you the basic criterion
Of what it means to be a true friend,
Reliant, accessible, and trusting.

Today: I spend time with the *Friend*.

Extravagant Persistence

You pester me to keep on growing
And, remarkably, persist in believing
In my inherent ability to be more.
At the same time, you continue
To love me, pretenses, warts, and all.
These continual nudges and urgings
Of yours furnish me with assurance
That you'll assist me in my changing.
Thank you Extravagant Persistence,
For never, ever, giving up on me.

Today: I trust that I can change.

Filler of Hearts

Rabindranath Tagore

O Filler of Hearts, what abundance,
What spiritual riches you contain.
You plead daily, "Wider, wider!
Unblock your constricted heart."
You consistently implore, "Open,
Open, open to receive my gifts."
When my heart does finally release
And receive your outpouring love,
Precious gifts come flowing forth
From your generous heart into mine.

Today: My heart opens a bit wider.

---✝---

The Way

John 14:6

We meet you in your gospel teachings,
Recognize you in the witness of your life,
Know you by the interior pathways
Leading us to love as you have done.
When we search for our bearings
Or question what is our true direction,
We can look to how you lived your years
And discern our own path for how to be.
Your lessons mark our lifelong journey
With constant signs of steady guidance.

Today: I look for signs of *The Way*.

---+---

Beloved Sculptor

Macrina Wiederkehr

In your loving hands, pliable clay takes shape.
The substance of something valuable comes alive.
What we might have rejected as worthless
Becomes a priceless form of hidden beauty.
Your vision of what now lies buried within life
Continues to develop in the shaping of ourselves.
Unwanted personality traits and tiresome troubles
Are received as teachers of spiritual development,
Accepted as unimagined profiles of needed wisdom
Sculpted by the dexterous movement of your love.

Today: I notice how I am influenced by *Beloved Sculptor*.

Giver of All

The Qur'an

We are the beggars who come to you,
Desiring to receive your boundless gifts.
We are the homeless with hungry eyes,
Waiting for your measure of handouts.
We are the powerless looking to you,
Searching for ways to be strengthened.
Giver of All, not every desire of ours is met.
Yet, countless, endless, are the large portions
You constantly bestow on those in need.
How wondrous is your nonstop generosity.

Today: I remember what I have received.

God

Your name on the lips of human history
Has inspired but also intimidated,
Has generated truth but also falsehood,
Has strengthened but also weakened,
Has transformed but also regressed.
So many interpret you as "theirs" alone
And act for their benefit but not for yours.
In spite of such misuse and false intention,
Your name continues to motivate saints
and prosper hope when all seems lost.

Today: I accept that *God* is more than mine.

FEBRUARY 13

Sanctuary

You are the trustworthy Sanctuary
For those living with any form of fear
Whether it be from within or without.
You are ready to be the safe haven
For those desiring a dwelling place
Where basic safety can be assured,
For those striving for secure peace
To replace hostility and violence,
And those who keep searching for someone
Who readily accepts them as they are.

Today: I yearn for all to find peace in the *Sanctuary*.

FEBRUARY 14

---+---

Love

1 John 4:16

You are the great heart of true loves,
Woven through the fabric of inner life.
You are the fondness in each genuine hug,
The spark and ardor of marital bliss,
The affection held in the eyes of a friend.
You move through parental tenderness
And those who carefully tend the weak.
You are knit into our unselfish actions,
Spun through each effort to be kind.
You are the one great Love in our loves.

Today: I find *Love* in my loves.

Eternal Presence

Psalm 139

The psalmist raises a hypothetical question:
"Where can I flee from your presence?"
And then proceeds to answer, "Nowhere"
For you are found in the highest of heavens
And in the lowest depths of the earth.
Who would want to run from you,
To escape your tremendous kindness?
Resistance might try to rule a wary heart
Or fear make an attempt to close off love,
But this does not keep you from staying near.

Today: I will not run from *Eternal Presence*.

---+---

Beauty Giver

"Beauty is in the eye of the beholder."
This we've heard from wise ones in the past.
You have given us perceptive eyes and ears
To discover what charms and gladdens us.
Everywhere beauty awaits our contemplation
In nature, music, art, word, drama, dance,
In human landscapes of body, mind, and soul.
To behold and receive these inspiring treasures
All we need do is awaken our dulled awareness
And bring a nonjudgmental openness of mind.

Today: With a grateful heart I find and receive beauty.

━━━━━━━━━━━━━━━┿━━━━━━━━━━━━━━━

Great Heart of Love

John 15:9

Could there be any love anywhere
More spacious than your heart?
Could there be any love anywhere
More warmly caring than your own?
Could there be any love anywhere
More ready to forgive, to delight?
Could there be any love anywhere
More devoted and unconditional?
Could it be that all truly kind love
Dwells within you, Great Heart of Love?

Today: My loving comes from the *Great Heart of Love*.

Master

Mark 1:21–22

The disciples grew in their understanding
And slowly began to call you Master,
The One sent to teach them the way.
They sensed the power of your authority,
Left all behind and leaned toward you.
Some days they found this easy to do
And sometimes they yearned to turn away.
I, too, slowly consent to your leadership,
To acknowledge the power of your teachings
And leave what hinders me from following.

Today: I keep my pompous ego from taking over.

FEBRUARY 19

Kindness

Titus 3:4–5

In sympathetic concern,
In gestures of helping,
In standing up for the weak,
In voicing affirmation,
In words of understanding,
In visits of solicitude,
In nonjudgmental thoughts,
In embraces of hospitality,
You touch us in human kindness
And hold us to your heart.

Today: I will be kind.

Sacred Source of Sleep

Edward Hays

Sleep, glorious sleep, mysterious sleep!
How remarkable that nightly moment
When sleep overtakes our consciousness
And slips us through the sleeve of rest,
When dreams arise to reach and teach,
And angels wrap their wings around us.
For all those nights and naps I've slept
As sweet and soundly as a contented baby,
Thank you, Sacred Source of Sleep,
For rest and renewal of body and spirit.

Today: Before I fall asleep, I give thanks for this gift.

Delight of My Heart

Oh, for those moments of unrestrained joy
When I sense the beauty of your presence,
Your ample arms wrapped warmly around me.
What gladness you signal in my dusty soul
Through quiet walks in nature's loveliness
Or easy conversations with a timeless friend.
Delight of My Heart, you bring such happiness
By your visitations of surprising pleasure.
They nurture what needs to thrive in me
And overtake what races toward desolation.

Today: I enjoy the *Delight of My Heart*.

Intimate Companion

You are the One to whom we can go
With the secrets and whispers inside us.
You are the One on whom we can lean
The most troubling of sorrows and woe.
You are the One in whom we confide
With the sureness of no cruel betrayal.
You are the One to whom we can turn
Resting securely in love deeply familiar.
You are the One who cherishes us fully,
Closer to us than we can ever imagine.

Today: My *Intimate Companion* abides with me.

Friend of
the Poor

The poor are everywhere,
Those society rejects or forgets.
You welcome them all.
You look toward. I look away.
You reach out. I hold back.
You accept fondly. I rebuff fearfully.
You give away. I clutch tightly.
You extend love. I offer pity.
When will I, too, go in your direction
And become a friend of the poor?

Today: I befriend those I reject or forget.

My Most Treasured Happiness

Karl Rahner

A lot of changes are required within me
Before I count you as my Most Treasured Happiness:
Unclasping my grip on what is unnecessary,
Releasing my aimless desire for the impossible,
Ceasing to clutch at things feeding my ego,
Forgiving long-held, musty grudges,
Turning from cultural notions of what satisfies.
All this, and much more, has to go on its way.
Only then will I realize who I have in you,
the source of what brings me true satisfaction.

Today: I realize who and what I have.

Old-Who

William Stafford

You are a "Who," and not a "What,"
A "Someone," and not a "Something."
"Old" you may be, surely beyond our time,
Past the ancient cliffs of human civilization.
Yet, you allow us the gift of communication,
The trickle of inner language, the silence
Of the unspoken to carry your messages.
Each of us, like the mystic poet Stafford,
Are lured into the mystery of your presence
And attempt again and again to speak with you.

Today: I communicate with *Old-Who*.

Divine Lover

Song of Songs 8:6–7

How far will I go to look for you?
How deep will I delve to know you?
How empty will I be to hold you?
How quiet will I be to perceive you?
How humble will I be to reach you?
How free will I be to accept you?
How open will I be to receive you?
How true will I be to love you?
How willing is this heart of mine
To pay the price to be one with you?

Today: I ask myself if I will pay the price.

✝

Castle of Resistance

John Micallef

When persuasive temptation looms large
And I struggle to choose what is right,
When I am too weak to voice a no
And feel obstinate pressure to give in
Rather than stand up for what is true,
I turn to you to find my needed strength.
For you are a fortified Castle of Resistance
Where the rooms abound with courage
And each hallway holds the armor of grace,
Always available to be put on and activated.

Today: I am aware of what tempts me from good.

Gentlest of Ways

Rainer Maria Rilke

Expectations of you to be harsh and demanding
Fade with the gospel reality of your gentleness:
Showing mercy to a sinner ready to be stoned,
Curing years of an ill woman's hemorrhaging,
Touching disdained lepers with tender concern,
Weeping at the gravesite of a beloved friend,
Awakening the dead, forgiving the arrogant,
Gathering playful children whom disciples shun.
Everywhere in your life there is tangible evidence
Confirming the truth of your gentle kind-heartedness.

Today: I approach all of life with gentleness.

March

We glimpse our own relative size in the universe and see that no human being can say who God should be or how God should act. We review our requirements of God and recognize them as our own fictions, things we tell ourselves to make ourselves feel safe or good or comfortable. Disillusioned, we find out what is not true and we are set free to seek what is—if we dare—to turn away from the God who was supposed to be in order to see the God who is.

Every letdown becomes a lesson and a lure. Did God fail to come when I rubbed the lantern? Then perhaps God is not a genie. Who, then, is God? Did God fail to punish my enemies? Then perhaps God is not a cop. Did God fail to make everything run smoothly? Then perhaps God is not a mechanic. Who, then, is God?

Over and over, my disappointments draw me deeper into the mystery of God's being and doing. Every time God declines to meet my expectations, another of my idols is exposed. Another curtain is drawn back so that I can see what I have propped up in God's place. No, that is not God. Who, then, is God? It is the question of a lifetime, and the answers are never big enough or finished. Pushing past curtain after curtain, it becomes clear that the failure is not God's but my own, for having such a poor and stingy imagination.

—*Barbara Brown Taylor*

Strength of Pilgrims

Dan Schutte

We each travel our internal Exodus,
Personal pilgrimages in the wilderness,
Sometimes voyages of our own making,
But mostly brought on by life's unfolding.
We wander, balking, hungry of heart,
Weakened in our desire to continue,
Searching for the home of our best self.
You offer your strength to us on the way,
Lifting us up when we stumble and fall,
Redirecting us when we lose the course.

Today: *Strength* for my journey is there for me.

MARCH 2

---✝---

Miracle Worker

Mark 1:29–34

The straightening of twisted limbs,
The healing of leprous wounds,
The quieting of a storm at sea,
The dead catching their breath,
None can compare to the miracles
You create within people's hearts.
Sinners choose to change their ways.
Hardened hearts finally soften.
Doubtful minds give way to faith,
And stubborn wills yield to your love.

Today: I open my entire being to the *Miracle Worker*.

My Salvation

Psalm 27:1

Contrary to the frequently quoted saying,
"God helps those who help themselves,"
Certain situations cannot be managed
No matter what we attempt to do.
At these times, we seek a full reprieve
At the welcome doorstep of your grace.
We call out amid our helpless affliction,
Begging relief from that which devours us,
Trusting you will lead us toward release
And help us break free from our captivity.

Today: I do what I can. Then I let go and trust.

Glorious One

Revelation 4:1–11

In the wisdom of aging friends,
In the sight of a shooting star,
In the play of waves upon the sea,
In the talent of artist and musician,
In the laughter of cheerful strangers,
In the touch of a faithful lover,
In the first sign of green after winter,
In the taste of Bread at the table,
In the haven of our own heart,
In these and more, we see your glory.

Today: I look for signs of the *Glorious One*.

✝

God of My Bitter Hours

Karl Rahner

Y ou knelt in the Gethsemane garden
In the final hours before your death,
The sweat of bloody regret on your brow.
We, too, have our painful episodes
When the bitter taste of obvious defeat
Barricades any hope of comfort and release.
You join us in our bitter hours of struggle
When opposition, discontent, or lament
Block the corridors to our peacefulness.
You reassure us, "This, too, will pass."

Today: I join my heart to the One in the garden.

MARCH 6

Encourager
of the Morning

Macrina Wiederkehr

The yawns, groans, and stretches
That come with first awakening
Reflect the mornings of my spirit.
There, too, I slowly become alert
To what requires my attentiveness.
You gently approach my drowsy self
Like a mother stirring her child awake,
Calling me from my sleep of indifference,
Insisting on my rising to your presence
And attentively greeting my inner light.

Today: I awaken to what sleeps in me.

God Who Breaks Chains

Elizabeth Johnson

I have been bound time and again
By fetters that shackled me tightly
And entangled my heart's desires.
These countless, vapid excuses of mine
For not being the person I could be
Have restrained the love in my heart
Intended to flow outward to others.
You continually show me these chains
And help me break loose, to be free
From whatever chokes my goodness.

Today: I pay attention to what chains me.

The Emptied One

Philippians 2:6–11

You often emptied yourself within ministry,
Giving of yourself fully for the sake of others.
You also suffered degradation and mockery,
Accepting the burden of the bloodied cross,
And made your way resolutely to Calvary.
Why did you not cling to your divine power?
Why allow your humanity to have full reign?
What kept you from running away from it all?
Were you teaching us, even through your dying,
That emptying out of self is part of the giving?

Today: I act out of love for the sake of others.

━━━━━━━━━━━━┼━━━━━━━━━━━━

Dweller in the Heart

Alakananda Devi

You inhabit the totality of my being
So quietly I often forget you are there.
You occupy the corners where even I
Sometimes fear to enter and reside.
You abide in the midst of my weakness
And accept my endless efforts to change.
Oh, the mystery, the wonder, the power
Of your dwelling within my simple heart!
Thank you for the gift of your presence,
For the permanent lodging of your love.

Today: I turn to the One who dwells in me.

---†---

Compassionate One

Luke 6:36

When did the people of your era distinguish you
As the person from whom compassion flowed?
Perhaps it was the way you touched a leper's hand
Or how you stopped to hear the widow's pain.
Maybe when you interrupted self-righteous men
And freed the frightened woman about to be stoned,
Or the tone of your voice when you responded
To the blind beggars' pleas to regain their sight.
Wherever you went, you moved closer to pain
Doing all you could to ease suffering and to heal.

Today: I learn how to care from the *Compassionate One*.

Divine Challenger

"When will you decide to truly listen?
How long will it take for you to forgive?
Have you considered being patient?
Are you judging that person fairly?
Does your honesty help or hurt?
What will it take for you to trust?
When will you cease your deception?
Do you know that I care about you?"
Ah, in so many ways you challenge us
Because you believe in who we can be.

Today: I follow through on a divine challenge.

One Who Weeps

Anselm Grün

Scripture tells twice of your weeping,
But undoubtedly there were other times
Besides your tears for a friend entombed
And a heartless city swept up in selfishness.
Surely your tender tears continue to emerge
As you look upon this hurting planet today.
Tears for children who are brutally betrayed
And every person's wrenching desolation,
Tears for the world's greed and plunder
And the careless way we treat one another.

Today: I renew my endeavor to be compassionate.

Christ

Mark 1:1–11

You are the Christ, the Anointed One,
Baptized in the Jordan by your cousin,
Hearing the beautiful word "Beloved"
Spoken of you by the divine Father.
What happened in the depths of yourself
When you heard such immense love
In that blessed moment of naming?
Did this designation awaken and stir in you
A desire to give your life in devoted service?
Did you know what a gift you would be?

Today: I do everything in a spirit of loving service.

Mother of the Weary

When we are worn from a day's work
Or bent beneath our suffering,
When we absorb the pain of another
Or tire from trying to do better,
When we are fatigued from reaching out
Or lose the strength to resist injustice,
You wrap your spacious maternal arms
Around our tiredness and affliction.
You cradle us with infinite compassion
And rock us gently with your love.

Today: I rest in the arms of the *Mother*.

The Subtle One

The Qur'an

Rarely do you communicate with us
Through exciting, burning-bush scenes.
Rather, you show up in our lives
In hushed, unobtrusive visitations,
Slowly penetrating our ordinariness
Like the quiet melting of spring snow.
Continue to teach us how near you are,
To trust in this truth although we do not see.
To love you, although we do not feel.
To speak with you, although we do not hear.

Today: I do not need a burning bush.

Silent Sentinel of My Soul

How closely you watch with me,
Silent in your careful observation,
Generous with your constant regard.
As vigilant as a night sentry on duty
Guarding prized treasures in a vault,
As careful as a concerned parent
Overseeing explorations of the child,
As quietly as the doting mother bird
Resting in the nest with her newborn,
So is your attentiveness to my soul.

Today: The *Silent Sentinel* guards my soul.

Healer

Psalm 107:17–22

We look to you for graceful balm,
Your medicine for our interior life.
Reach toward our old heartaches.
Help us to end what causes distress,
To release what stunts our growth
In becoming all we are meant to be.
Show us our troublesome blind spots
So we are not secretly ruled by them.
Touch the soreness of our spirit
And heal us of our inner ailments.

Today: I bring what hurts in me to the *Healer*.

Consoler

2 Corinthians 1:3–4

You remain our core consolation
When depression digs deeply
Into the remains of our energy,
When loss obliterates our joy
And emptiness predominates,
When turmoil rules our mind
Or disappointment engulfs us.
You are a gentle touch of kindness,
A soothing word of genuine support,
A strengthening hug of sympathy.

Today: The *Consoler* abides with me.

Deliverer

Psalm 18:16–19

Deliver us
From restless anxiety and impatience,
From the desire to dominate others,
From disregard for those in need,
From seeking to be the perfect one,
From destructive, gossiping words,
From immersion in selfish ambition,
From self-pity and self-doubt,
From intolerance of others' faults,
From all that attempts to destroy love.

Today: I pray for my deliverance.

Mother Hen

Matthew 23:37

Like a Mother Hen with chicks
You attentively care for us,
Gathering us under your wing,
Feeding us with wisdom,
Protecting us from harm,
Nursing our wounds,
Teaching us responsibility,
Leading us on the way,
Expecting us to follow,
Trusting us to grow up.

Today: I find a home under *Mother Hen's* wing.

---+---

Core of Community

Acts 2:43–47

With you as the nucleus
Of every group that gathers,
Differences are respected
And tensions are overcome.
Those speaking from the edge
Gain a listening ear.
Compassion thrives.
Egos maintain a low profile.
With you as Core of Community
Peace abides and love abounds.

Today: The *Core of Community* affects my relationships.

Liberator God

Edward Hays

How often we find ourselves
In a prison of our own making,
Held by resentment and hostility
Or cultural pressures to look good,
Pressed by the need to be right,
Caught up in heartless criticism
Or useless apprehensions.
You free us from one prison cell,
But then we move to another.
Help us to be fully liberated.

Today: I leave behind something that imprisons me.

Shekinah

Jewish

Oh, the power of your steady presence
Sweeping through the soul's journey!
Although you are invisible and unseen
You come to dwell among the people
As a guide through the long wilderness,
A light of assurance and remembrance.
Your spirit resides in the Tabernacle
And in meeting places of soul with divinity.
In you, Shekinah, is found the paradox
Of your remoteness and your nearness.

Today: *Shekinah* resides within the tabernacle of myself.

---+---

My Help

Psalm 121:2

Looking back on my life
I cannot count the times
I've called for your aid.
Looking back on my life
I cannot count the times
You were there for me.
Looking back on my life
I cannot count the times
When I forgot you were near,
And fell into the pit of my woes.

Today: When I need *My Help*, I call out.

Gracious Creator

Edward Hays

Today, at this precise moment,
The effects of your graciousness
Are evident throughout my body.
My countless cells keep changing
As my strength and health renew.
My heart beats it's steady rhythm.
My lungs securely breathe in air.
My whole being responds with ease,
Nurtured by your creative love.
My thankful spirit fills with wonder.

Today: I am grateful to my *Gracious Creator*.

Necessary Being

Beatrice Bruteau

You comfort me
When I am hurting.
You draw me to others
When I am loving.
You inspire me
When I am rejoicing.
You encourage me
When I am growing.
You are always there.
Do I need you? Oh, yes!

Today: I recognize my need.

Voice of Freedom

Calling softly to my secret self.
Offering space to try again.
Asking trust when I cave in to fear.
Urging me to stand with strength.
Whispering daily encouragement.
Pleading with me to take risks.
Warning when I am in trouble.
Affirming belief in my endeavors.
Reminding me time and again
To liberate my wings of goodness.

Today: I listen.

---†---

Servant of Others

John 13:16

You lovingly washed your disciples' feet,
Dirty, smelly as they must have been.
And I, who want to be of service
So quickly turn away from the difficult,
Try to ease my way out of anything
That takes too much of my precious time
Or asks more than I am wanting to give.
When will I come to accept the reality
That following your example of service
Requires more than seeking my own comfort?

Today: I act in accordance with the *Servant of Others*.

The Crucified

John 19:17–23

Once on the cross, more than enough.
But your crucifixion goes on today
In killings, rapes, and war devastation,
Innocent ones maimed and abused,
Martyred ones speaking out for justice,
Brave ones protecting the defenseless,
All those men and women who die
Working tirelessly for the good of others.
When will your crucifixion end?
Not until everyone is a person of love.

Today: I live as a person of love.

---†---

Fountain of Mercy

Edward Hays

You would pour your flowing love
Profusely upon my calloused deeds
And rinse them with your forgiveness.
But I would prefer to blame others
Than to acknowledge my own faults.
I would rather look away in denial
Than look toward my actual omissions.
I would choose to forget my offenses
Instead of admitting I have done wrong.
Yet, you remain a Fountain of Mercy.

Today: I bathe in the *Fountain of Mercy*.

Lamb of God

John 1:35–36

Your cousin John looked upon you
With clear eyes that penetrated deeply.
"Behold the Lamb of God," John pronounced
As he singled you out with admiration,
Inviting all to see what his inner eye saw.
When John beheld your boundless compassion
He knew you were able to give your life freely.
For he observed what others had not seen:
A strong, courageous, loving human being
Willing to speak the truth openly to all.

Today: I behold the *Lamb of God* with my inner eye.

April

In the scripture Jesus studied as a child, God appeared to Moses in the form of a burning bush. "What is your name?" Moses asked. And God answered Moses, "I AM WHO I AM."

Of all the glorious names for the Divine—King of Kings, Great Spirit, Allah, Mother Goddess—to say only "I am who I am" seems simple and honest. The Jews never spoke God's name aloud, recognizing that any name makes God too small. Some Jewish scholars prefer "I will be who I will be." Here, there is a sense of God unfolding and evolving by our side, discovered in a thousand unexpected revelations. With such a name, God can be discovered anywhere.

All scripture is a treasure of stories collected, in the end, to paint a picture of the nature of God. There is no single name large enough, and so we tell everything, every moment where God is seen, felt, tasted. What can we possibly leave out? The list is too long; it takes an entire human life just to say it.

—*Wayne Muller*

APRIL 1

Serene One

Nan Merrill

In you is found no fussing or fluster.
Genuine peacefulness resides in you.
Your tranquility comes from knowing
All is as it is and all is as it will be.
You remain unruffled and patient,
Continually drawing us toward you
So we can release our restlessness
And relinquish our needless anxiety.
As we learn to place our trust in you,
Our serenity gradually mirrors your own.

Today: I find peace in trusting the *Serene One*.

---†---

Redeemer

Psalm 19:14

You are the One sent to free us
From inner and outer oppression,
To liberate us from our illusions
And anything taking us from you,
Assisting us to recover our ability
To be people of loving kindness.
You have shown us the clear way
And have loved us back into life.
You will wait for as long as it takes
For us to accept your gift of freedom.

Today: I give myself to the *Redeemer*.

Lion

Revelation 5:5

A power to be respected.
A voice obliging attention.
An energy of rippling effect.
A beauty to be admired.
A fierceness that protects.
A ruler requiring obedience.
Like creatures of the savanna,
You are in charge of the pride.
The long strides of your love
Run to embrace all creation.

Today: The *Lion's* energy stirs me toward good.

APRIL 4

Shepherd

Psalm 23

I have been in that bleak valley
When the last bit of joyfulness
Was sucked out of my spirit
By the ripping winds of desolation.
In those times of extended anguish
The memory of green pastures
With you shepherding my way
Brought me strength to go on.
Shepherd, now, others in need
As they stumble on their dark road.

Today: I unite my heart with those in gloomy valleys.

Lord of All Eagerness

Jan Struther

When our will dances
In sync with your own,
And our mind vibrates
With enthusiasm
For your teachings,
When our entire self
Ardently embraces you,
Then it becomes evident
That our passion for you
Reflects your eagerness for us.

Today: I restore my eagerness for spiritual growth.

Flute Player

Hafiz

You are the Pied Piper
Of our creaturely hearts.
Your clear, enticing music
Wafts melodiously for us,
A serenade of devoted love
Played from birth to death.
But the clutter oppressing
Our minds and hearts
Prevents us from hearing
This enchanting song of yours.

Today: I listen to the *Flute Player's* serenade.

APRIL 7

Source of All Being

Carmelite Breviary

Source of existence.
Source of wisdom.
Source of hope.
Source of compassion.
Source of desire for good.
Source of unselfish love.
Source of prayer.
Source of justice.
Source of eternal life.
Source of all that I am.

Today: I commune with my *Source*.

✝

Hearer of All

The Qur'an

You hear the jubilation
Of the happy-hearted,
And the questioning
Of the confused seeker.
You hear the shout
Of the angry one
And the last sigh
Of the dying.
The ear of your heart
Is always open to us.

Today: The *Hearer of All* listens to me.

---✝---

Joy of Our Desiring

Martin Jahn

Every creature desires happiness.
Each one longs for contentment
And an ongoing sense of well-being.
You are the true Joy of Our Desiring
Although we may not recognize this.
Beneath our longing and yearning
Your presence of ceaseless delight
Waits for us to identify what is ours.
Help us find in our joys and pleasures
The deeper joy of yourself within them.

Today: My heart focuses on true *Joy*.

Lord of the Dance

Sydney B. Carter

Invite me to dance.
Lead the way.
Teach me the steps
And I will follow you.
Twirl me around wildly
Or do a slow glide.
Whatever the form
I will remain in step,
Heeding the gestures
Of your graced movement.

Today: I let the *Lord of the Dance* lead me.

APRIL 11

---†---

Pardoner

Karl Rahner

I have stood before you
On numerous occasions,
Knowing my transgression,
Guilty, fairly convicted.
You reach out mercifully,
Drawing my regret toward you
With a generous reception.
In that moment of pardon
The falseness in my life
Dissolves in your tenderness.

Today: I accept the divine pardon offered to me.

The Disturber

Wake us up
To what needs doing,
And what needs undoing.
Wake us up
To what must be let go,
And what to draw closer.
Wake us up to what enlarges love
And what diminishes it.
In all parts of our life,
Disturb and wake us up!

Today: I become wider awake.

APRIL 13

Beautiful Presence

Macrina Wiederkehr

How often I savor your presence
In the toss and turn of my everyday life.
The little moments of recognition
That bring me home to your beauty.
The kind gestures of thoughtfulness
That touch me in life's turbulence.
The enriching, nurturing experiences
That renew and enliven my spirit.
And the ways you make yourself known
In the loveliness of nature's diversity.

Today: I am attentive to *Beautiful Presence*.

Savior

Luke 2:8–11

Save us from all that keeps us
From giving our hearts to you.
Save us from all that restrains us
From sharing our love with others.
Save us from all that deceives us
By diversion and self-centeredness.
Save us from all that entices us
Into conscious, destructive deeds.
Save us from ignorance of our worth
And from choosing to live our life fully.

Today: I see what needs saving in my life.

Hidden One

Even though you are fully present
I do not always detect your nearness.
I look for you, anticipate you,
Listen for a hint of your voice
Like a tulip bulb in placid soil
Waiting for the call to rise up.
You will reveal yourself in due season.
In the meantime, I walk in faith,
Trusting you are in the heart of life,
Secreted in darkness but ever present.

Today: I have faith in divine hiddenness.

The Magnificent

The Qur'an

I honor and praise you, Magnificent One,
For your awe-inspiring works of wonder.
For your glorious flinging of stars
Into the depths of our vast universe.
For your persistent, careful sculpting
Of hearts of stone into hearts of flesh.
For your willingness to carry our pain
And strengthen our hope for healing.
For your astounding resourcefulness
Enriching our lives with your goodness.

Today: I offer praise to *The Magnificent*.

Tomb-Opener

John 11:38–44

Just when the smell of death
Becomes unbearable
And the huge stone blocking light
Seems unmovable,
You send your angels in disguise
To let in light and refresh the air.
And in our returning to life
We discover that some blockages
Are far too massive
For us to remove by ourselves.

Today: I am ready to be untombed.

———————————— ┼ ————————————

The Restorer

The Qur'an

At times my relationship with you
Is like a shabby piece of furniture
With the worn wood losing its luster,
Obviously in need of refurbishment
After years of thoughtless negligence.
You help me clean, polish, and repair
My faded prayer and drab behavior.
You work with me until I come clean,
Restoring the original sheen of my spirit
Until once again I reflect your beauty.

Today: I notice what might need restoring.

Drifting Mist

Rainer Maria Rilke

The mist that floats over the valley
Drifts along without a morning voice.
It cannot be caught or contained
As it sails with ease and touches all,
Leaving the effects of its moist breath
On each stem of grass and every stone.
Your presence glides in similar fashion.
Like the soft mist touching all it reaches
You also leave the quiet, soft memory
Of your gentle presence in our lives.

Today: *Drifting Mist* floats through my day.

Guardian of
My Deepest Self

You are the watchful Guardian
Of that most vulnerable self
Which resides deep inside,
Where we are easily affected
By what others say and do,
Where our self-esteem is slain
By outbursts of insult and shame.
There in that defenseless place
You continually furnish reminders
Of what is good and true in us.

Today: I listen to my *Guardian*'s reminders.

Radiant Rain God

Edward Hays

You come to us unexpectedly
Like a sudden April rainfall
Drenching newly planted flowers.
You rinse the neglected residue
From our wearied, worn spirits
And refresh our tired desire
To give ourselves fully to you.
The steady patter of your love
Upon the garden of our hearts
Activates what is best in us.

Today: I welcome refreshing *Rain*.

Mother of Earth

You embrace each element of the planet
As a much-loved child held to the breast,
Concerned about each one's well-being
And how your beloved planet is treated.
You are ever present as the nurturer of life
And a companion with what eventually dies.
You embrace the pattern of the seasons
With their natural unfolding transformation
And weep in sorrow for what becomes extinct
When humanity carelessly hurries its death.

Today: I care for our planet by how I live.

The Patient One

The Qur'an

You patiently wait for me to return
When I get sidetracked in my problems
Or endlessly absorbed in useless fretting.
You lovingly continue to watch over me
When I get mired in my selfish endeavors
Or rigidly stand in concreted defensiveness.
You continue to believe in my potential
Even when I deliberately avoid using my talents
Or shove aside what is meant for my growth.
Your patience tells me of your great love.

Today: I practice being patient with others.

Hallowing of My Acts

Karl Rahner

You breathe on my attempts
To be a person of kindness.
You touch my soiled efforts
To reach out in forgiveness.
You hold carefully my desire
To offer comfort and care.
You receive my every prayer
No matter how crumpled it is.
You give all of this a sacred hue,
A liberal blessing of your love.

Today: My actions are hallowed when done lovingly.

Risen Christ

John 21:1–19

No one expected your return.
You astonished your disciples
When you slipped from the tomb.
You came extending peace,
Offering forgiveness for denial,
Extending faith to the doubtful.
You met them at the seashore
And on the road toward home.
Each one's grieving heart overjoyed.
Each one's closed mind opened wide.

Today: I let myself be astonished.

Vine

John 15:5

When I reflect on the people
Whom I dislike and tend to avoid,
The people whose aberrant behavior
Leads me to think less of them,
Then I remember who you are:
The true Vine, the anchor of love
To which every person is joined.
You draw each of us to yourself
Regardless of who or how we are.
If I am with you, then so are they.

Today: I turn my heart toward *all* people.

Hope Through the Ages

Shannon Wexelberg

When death stalks us
And troubles rage on,
When affection wavers
And people fail us,
When light grows faint
And darkness expands,
When all seems useless,
And nothing is left,
You remain by our side,
Our true and lasting love.

Today: I reflect on what my hope is.

Inspirer
of Faith

The Qur'an

Your love expressed through others
Inspires my faith.
Your beauty reflected in creation
Inspires my faith.
Your presence within Eucharist
Inspires my faith.
Your justice shown in leadership
Inspires my faith.
In countless surprising sources
You help me believe in you.

Today: I recognize my sources of inspiration.

┼

The Resurrection

John 11:25

Like a seed trampled underfoot,
You overcame violence and took root.
Like a flower wilted by a freeze,
You lifted your head and newly bloomed.
Like a stream gone dry in drought,
You sought the source and survived.
Like a tree bent over from the storm,
You stood up straight and tall again.
Like a faithful lover returning home,
I welcome your risen presence now.

Today: I welcome the *Resurrected One*.

Rainmaker

Sri Lankan

Seed the empty clouds of my heart
With a downpour of your love.
Gather the raindrops of joyfulness
And rinse away my melancholy.
Shower the land of my mind
With thoughts beneficial to all.
Sprinkle true motivation through
The charitable deeds that I do.
Water my efforts at forgiveness
With the flowing rains of compassion.

Today: The *Rainmaker* seeds my heart.

May

Once when I was preparing to spend a period of time in a hermitage, I found myself spontaneously writing. The words tumbled from deep within me: "When I asked my God if I could come and stay with Him for awhile, She said: Yes, but don't bring your God with you."

Oh, how easy it is to clutter up the path of the Holy Spirit with my images and preconceptions of God! The mystical heart lets go of all images, icons, and expectations of God. The mystical heart is ever pregnant with the possibility of God. The mystical heart waits in awe for the revelation of God in every single moment.

—*Edwina Gateley*

MAY 1

Breath of Life

Genesis 2:7

Could I live without you?
No more than I can exist
Without oxygen for my lungs.
You sustain my pulse of life
Both internally and externally.
Each breath of your love
Rejuvenates my spirit.
You sustain my daily rhythm
Of being a loving presence
In all I am and all I do.

Today: I breathe in divine love.

┼

Holy Mother

Edward Hays

Cradle us.
Comfort us.
Nurture us.
Teach us.
Protect us.
Forgive us.
Counsel us.
Celebrate us.
Sustain us.
Love us.

Today: I turn with gratitude to *Holy Mother*.

MAY 3

＋

Inspiring Spirit

1 Corinthians 12:4–11

Your powerful breath of grace
Circles through my days and nights.
You drift in with robust insights,
Chase out days of foggy dullness.
You blow in strongly after a storm
Clearing out my emotional space.
You soar in with helpful dreams
To restore my purpose and direction.
You breeze in on calming winds
Bringing comfort and peacefulness.

Today: *Inspiring Spirit* moves within my mind and heart.

Living Water

John 4:13

A rainfall of your love
Seeps into parched spirits.
A shower of your kindness
Soaks dried out caring.
A sprinkle of your grace
Moistens hardened grudges.
A stream of your comfort
Softens endless hurts.
A deluge of your peace
Washes away irritability.

Today: *Living Water* washes over me.

Guide to Repentance

The Qur'an

Lead me to see clearly
When I need to truly repent
And when the guilt I feel
Is not helpful for my growth.
Guide me to change my heart
When I have gone astray.
Draw me into genuine sorrow
For my deliberate wrongdoings.
Strengthen my inner resolve
To be a person of great love.

Today: I resolve to change what keeps me from loving.

Morning Star

Easter Exultet

O Morning Star,
Glimmering on the curve
Of night, a steady presence
Calling my heart to arise
Into the brightness of dawn!
You gladden my spirit
And sweeten my disposition
As I greet the opening day.
I rise from my sleepiness
With the fullness of your hope.

Today: I carry hope in my heart.

Life

John 14:6

Like the unfolding of a fern
Or the leafing of a tree,
Like a steady mountain stream
Or strong waves of the sea,
Like a heart carrying blood
To all parts of the body,
So you are present in us.
You course through the veins
Of our souls, of our lives,
Energizing our spiritual growth.

Today: I sense *Life* pulsing in my being.

Word of Gladness

Bernadette Farrell

We know you, Word of Gladness,
Through our lives and in your voice:
"Do not let your hearts be troubled.
Come to me, all who are weary.
My peace I give to you.
You are the light of the world.
I will be with you.
Do not weep.
Your sins are forgiven.
Search, and you will find."

Today: I welcome the *Word of Gladness*.

———————————————— ✝ ————————————————

Secret One

Mary Southard

Secret One, hidden in the subways
Where homeless people dwell.
Concealed in the faces of enemies
We've never met except in the news.
Disguised among our neighbors
Who rankle, offend, and annoy us.
Unnoticed in the gift of sacraments
When the eyes of our heart are veiled.
Only with the obscured view of faith
And an open spirit do we glimpse you.

Today: I look with faith for the *Secret One*.

The Guest

Eleanor Farjeon

How do I welcome you
Guest of my heart?
Do I pay attention to you,
Offer you a cup of tea,
Enter into communication?
Or do I leave you sitting alone
While I go busily onward,
Feeling I've done my duty
By simply opening the door
And inviting you in?

Today: I do more than open the door.

Flower of Love

Dan Schutte

You are the bud in relationships
Newly found and enjoyed.
You are the petals of generosity
Expanding in the heart.
You are the full bloom of care
Shaped through selflessness.
You are the color of goodness
Growing in the inner garden.
You are, for each of us,
The flower that never fades.

Today: I tend the garden of *Love*.

✛

Feast Giver

Luke 14:15–24

Each day I am invited to come
And share in your banquet,
To receive from your table of love
Spiritual bounty for my deepest self.
What keeps me from accepting?
What holds me back from partaking?
Do I not believe in your nourishment?
Am I overly engaged elsewhere?
How could I not come forth with joy
And dine in your graced presence?

Today: I accept the *Feast Giver's* invitation.

┼

Source of Amazement

I am sometimes seized by wonder
At daily marvels large and small,
Birthing, living, loving, playing,
Things amazing, awesome, splendid.
They zap my overly full mind into alertness
And refresh my dull connection with you.
Thank you for the regular reminders
That come sailing out of nowhere.
These gifts let me slow my harried breath
And cause me to wipe happy tears of wonder.

Today: I notice something that amazes me.

Soul Liberator

Come with your freeing love
And unburden my barnacled soul,
That precious, pure essence,
The enduring core of my self.
Come, release the false clutches,
Those stifling cultural fallacies
And adhering, personal deceptions
That prevent me from being true.
Liberate all that hampers me
From living authentically.

Today: I get in touch with my falseness.

⊢⊣

God of the Gentle Wind and Terrible Battles

Karl Rahner

In the fierce forces of life
And in the tender touches,
In the harshest experience
And most genial welcome,
In excruciating discord
And in deepest harmony,
In the battle for good health
And the slip into final death,
You do not discriminate
On being present with us.

Today: No matter how I feel, I trust I am not alone.

Carrier of Memories

Deuteronomy 4:9

When we are distracted or disenchanted
You keep custody of our priceless memories,
The stories of our association with you:
Remembrances of your enduring love
When we wandered far away from you
And you never once gave up on us,
When we doubted our self-worth
And you patiently led us to our goodness,
When we felt the harsh blows of life
And you held out your arms to embrace us.

Today: I recall a hope-filled memory.

Lord of All Calm

Jan Struther

You bring durability like mountains
And tranquility gentle as a violet.
You are continually available
For us to turn toward, to find peace,
To locate a place to rest our heart
With its endless preoccupations.
When anxiety floods our mind
And disrupts the flow of serenity,
You await our receptivity to you
So we can receive your stillness.

Today: I locate calmness amid what distracts me.

Holy Spirit

2 Corinthians 3:17–18

Unlike the apprehensive disciples locked
In the Upper Room with their fears,
I *do* have expectations of your coming.
Yet, you continue to surprise me, too.
I anticipate your entrance as a wild gust
And then you slip quietly into my life.
I wait for you to speak instantly,
Instead, you slowly share your guidance.
I look for you in the highly unusual
And, of course, you show up in the ordinary.

Today: I let myself be surprised by the *Holy Spirit*.

Gracious Gardener

Genesis 2:8

We are your cultivated garden,
You, the Gracious Gardener.
You plant loving kindness in us
And diligently watch over it,
Watering it daily with grace
And waiting for growth to follow.
You weed out what is destructive
And shore up what is fragile.
You rejoice in the garden's produce,
Harvesting it with immense delight.

Today: I notice what is growing in my inner garden.

Transforming Presence

You are more than the softening touch
Placed upon our calloused hearts.
You are the constant tumbling waves
Slowly smoothing our roughened stones.
You are yeast within the flour of sorrows
Enabling our lost happiness to rise again.
You are spirit-filled chlorophyll
Greening our ever-developing virtues.
Wherever you make your dwelling,
Necessary change is ready to follow.

Today: I visit my inner sites of transformation.

Home of Good Choices

Whether to keep or let go,
To reach out or pull back,
To rest or keep going,
To speak out or be silent,
To forgive or stay angry,
To offer help or turn away.
These choices and more
Tumble and spin around in us.
If we bring them to you,
We will make wise decisions.

Today: I include my *Home* in decision-making.

┼

Stealer of Hearts

Hindu

You're very clever at it,
How you slip inside a prayer
Or enter a life unannounced
And claim a heart for your own.
In the flutter of an eyelid,
A long yawn or a deep breath,
Whoosh, you steal them away.
Sometimes the process is slow
But you never stop pilfering.
Come snatch my heart anytime!

Today: I give my heart willingly.

Anointed One

Luke 7:37–38

It was women who anointed you.
One used expensive, fragrant oil
To pour forth freely over your head.
Another bathed your feet with tears
And touched them with her sorrow.
Each one's action a silent message
Of devoted love, a recognition
That your heart was wide enough,
Humble enough, exposed enough,
To receive from both saint and sinner.

Today: I anoint all I meet with my kindness.

MAY 24

✝

Tender Sister

Bernadette Farrell

Joining hands, joining hearts.
You know me like no other.
My secrets slipped inside your ear.
My dreams tucked into your heart.
My every joy linked with yours.
With you I can enter life's woes.
With you I can laugh heartily.
With you I can accept challenge.
In all my moods and voices
I know you will listen and advise.

Today: I link my heart to the *Tender Sister*.

$$+$$

Wind

Acts 2:1–4

Suddenly, without warning,
The burst of your presence
Floods the room. Then,
An entire house fills with power.
The intensity of your nearness
Releases the prisoners of fear
And opens their hearts wide.
Each one is filled with your breath.
Astonished and empowered,
New abilities arise within them.

Today: I breathe in the *Wind*.

Guide of My Life

Psalm 86:11

How quickly I sink into selfish trenches
Created by my mismanaged ego.
How easily I slide into harsh judgments
Harbored in my critical mind.
How fully I fall into patterns of pride
Nurtured by my need to be right.
Come release me, Guide of My Life.
Reveal again the accurate direction.
Turn my heart toward your golden path.
Activate the love that sleeps in me.

Today: I turn toward my inner *Guide*.

Lily of the Valley

Anita Price Baird

Such powerful fragrance
From one tiny, humble flower.
A whiff of its intense sweetness
Absorbs my complete attention.
So it is with your divine essence.
One whiff, one brief encounter,
Only this much is necessary
To restore spiritual balance.
Remembrance of your aroma
Lingers long and lovingly with me.

Today: I breathe the fragrance of the *Lily*.

Source of All Our Store

Veni Sancte Spiritus

You store your bounty within us,
Entrusting it to our safe keeping.
Boxes of unconditional love.
Suitcases of patience and joy.
Cupboards that contain peace.
Closets bursting with charity.
Sacks filled with unselfishness.
Cartons containing faithfulness.
And big packages of self-control.
When will we decide to open them?

Today: I deliberately share from the *Source*.

Spirit of Putter

Kathy Reardon

Slow me from the frantic pace.
Help me halt the constant pressure
Of getting the hurried things done.
Let me dawdle the day away,
Ease into the morning snail-like.
Savor what I usually zoom by,
Tinker with stuff here and there.
And at the end of the idle day
Let me be content with doing nothing
Except enjoying my time with you.

Today: I'll not feel guilty about slowing down.

Spirit of InterBeing

Paul F. Knitter

There is no separation from you,
No disconnection or apartness.
There is no place where you are not,
No inner sanctum without your life.
When the breath of creation fills us,
You move as an intricate part of our being.
Every sacrament of life invites a reminder
Of how deeply wedded we are to you,
Each situation contains an opportunity
To engage with this profound oneness.

Today: I reflect on my unity with *Spirit of InterBeing*.

MAY 31

My Portion

Psalm 16:5

Could I ever truly understand
How much I receive from you?
The fullness of your great love,
The splendor of your creation,
The goodness of your people,
The bounty of your daily grace.
Every day upon my awaking
I receive the bequest of gifts
That I never could have earned.
Given because of your generosity.

Today: I gratefully accept my *Portion*.

June

The first expression of the unknowability of God is the proliferation of names, images, and concepts, each of which provides a different perspective onto divine excellence. For if we were able to see into the very essence of God and wrap our minds around this, we would be able to express the divine by only one, straight-as-an-arrow name. As created beings, however, we can never do this. Instead, the diversity of the world offers fragments of beauty, goodness, and truth, both social and cosmic, facets of reality that point us in different ways to the one ineffable source and goal of all. None alone or even all taken together can exhaust the reality of divine mystery. Each symbol has a unique intelligibility that adds its own significance to the small store of collected human wisdom about the divine.

—Elizabeth Johnson

Radiant Eye of Longing in My Breast

Rabia al-Adawiyya

This stirring in my distracted heart,
The movement of love's awakening,
This return to my essential trueness,
The growing desire for communion,
All this emergent yearning is from you.
Like a diamond sparkling in sunlight
So are you in the center of my depths,
Leading, drawing, urging, coaxing,
Alluring me as I find my way to you,
Toward the jewel of your exquisite love.

Today: I am drawn to the *Radiant Eye of Longing*.

JUNE 2

✝

Solace

Veni Sancte Spiritus

You support and console us.
The disheartened you encourage.
The depressed you hold close.
The displaced you bring home.
The disregarded you give esteem.
The disabled you offer support.
The disturbed you extend peace.
The disgruntled you cheer up.
The disillusioned you enlighten.
The disappointed you reassure.

Today: I bring *Solace* with me.

┼

Beloved

Mark 9:2–8

In a mystical moment on a mountain top
You are addressed in a most precious way.
Suitable for one entwined with divinity
Whose affectionate spirit touches all.
Was it out of this mystical experience
That you approached the forsaken ones
With a gaze that spoke the same thing?
Would that all of us fully understood
That each person is your "beloved,"
Cherished and reverenced in your heart.

Today: I bring those who feel unloved to the *Beloved*.

Bough of Blessing

Dan Schutte

I sit beneath your tree of life
Receiving the green aliveness.
The unseen energy of your love
Sings in me like photosynthesis
Making music in the happy leaves.
My years with you gather round me
Humming a history of your kindness.
On no day have you ever forsaken me.
In every year you have been there
Greening my life with your grace.

Today: I live with a grateful heart.

Light

You contain a tableau of possibilities,
Countless opportunities to encounter
Your indwelling gift of radiance.
A glimmer of hope in depression.
A ray of courage amid life's trials.
A sparkle of joy at the end of illness.
A flash of valuable intuition.
A beam of illuminating perception.
A glow of pleasure and contentment.
A radiance only the stilled soul perceives.

Today: I am aware of my inner *Light*.

Blessed Trinity

Matthew 28:19

It is impossible to rationally unravel
The mystery of your eternal unity.
I ponder "persons, personalities,
One community of eternal love"
But these acceptable theologies
Quickly wear thin in my inner domain.
So I decide to view you another way:
Three dancing spheres of pure love
Entwined with ribbons of spun gold,
Threading through everything that exists.

Today: Ribbons of golden love dance in my heart.

Force of Life

Mark Nepo

Like strong grass pushing itself upward
Between thick layers of concrete sidewalk
Or the sun refusing to stay behind clouds.
Like the push of water in a flowing spring
Or the urgent, pressing contractions of birth.
Like the stubborn oak leaves of last autumn
Shoved off by spring's burst of budding life.
So are you spiritual vigor and strong energy
Forever present within our hidden selves,
Sustaining and growing us into deep love.

Today: I acknowledge the *Force of Life* within me.

Eternal Flame

Bernadette Farrell

When I search for light in my darkness,
You are there.
When I experience the star-filled universe,
You are there.
When I long for warmth in cold relationships,
You are there.
When I wonder what will sustain my faith,
You are there.
When I appreciate faithfulness of old friends,
You are there.

Today: The *Eternal Flame* keeps my hope alive.

Balm to the Weary

Rabindranath Tagore

The soothing of your compassion
Eases my heart's tiredness
And touches the wounded places.
The ointment of your care
Seeps into the worn-out muscles
Of my overly extended schedule.
The salve of your understanding
Revives my exhausted patience.
The gentle massage of your love
Restores my depleted kindness.

Today: I accept the *Balm* offered to me.

╬

Font of Knowledge

Dan Schutte

From you is contained the truth
Of how to live our lives well.
Live simply. Go the extra mile.
Do not judge. Give generously.
Respect self and others. Rest.
Love unconditionally. Forgive.
This wisdom and much more
You offer for our spiritual benefit.
It is left to us to drink fully
From you, our Font of Knowledge.

Today: I respond to the *Knowledge* given to me.

Desire of the Everlasting Hills

Litany of the Sacred Heart

Creation echoes your kinship of love.
You call to us throughout the ages
In jubilant song of the ancient psalmist
Who has the hills singing exultantly.
With one voice they joyfully acknowledge
Your resonance in the heart of nature.
O Desire of the Everlasting Hills,
You dance, too, in the story of our lives
With the rhythm of your loving heartbeat.
May we increase our receptivity to you.

Today: I open my heart to *Desire of the Everlasting Hills.*

Doorkeeper of the Heart

Rabia al-Adawiyya

How grateful I am for your help
As the Doorkeeper of my heart.
Much riff-raff attempts to enter,
To slip by your alert, careful eye.
You serve as the attentive sentry,
Sorting out what comes and goes,
Welcoming what helps me grow
And warning of what will injure.
It is only when I ignore your voice
That damaging entries get inside.

Today: Only helpful visitors are allowed in my heart.

Sacred Heart

Yours is the full Heart of acceptance
Welcoming those pushed to the edge.
The Heart overflowing with concern,
Touching the bereaved and the ill.
The Heart broken open and bruised
Hurting from those who reject you.
The Heart peaceful and trusting
Praying alone in hillside solitude.
Yours is the Heart wider than an ocean
Inviting every person into unity with you.

Today: I open my heart to the *Sacred Heart*.

Sender

Isaiah 6:1–8

Not only those in scripture are sent.
You also dispatch each one of us
To be an eager messenger of your love.
"Go!" you say, "Do not be afraid.
I have imperative work for you to do.
Keep your mind's eye focused on me.
Bring my teachings of love into your life."
Slowly we learn that what you desire
Is not worldly success but faithfulness,
Not ego elation but dedicated service.

Today: I am ready to be sent.

Father of the Poor

Veni Sancte Spiritus

You provide the poorest of poor with a home,
A compassionate haven in your heart of love.
How you must long to clothe and feed them,
To visit the many disregarded and forgotten,
To comfort the countless rejected each day,
To provide the hungry what is rightfully theirs.
You look to us to be your presence for them,
To bring our skills, share our time, offer our care
In alleviating the pain of those who have little.
You ask us to join you in diminishing their poverty.

Today: I pray for commitment to those who are poor.

Snatcher of Fire

Laurens van der Post

I imagine how you stealthily enter
The lit hearth of early humankind,
Capturing a small flame from the fire
And gleefully storing it in your heart.
There it merges with your great love
To be forever a blaze of devotion,
A blend of warmth, passion, and zeal.
No wonder the flame of Pentecost
Ignited the disciples into ardent action.
You instill our hearts with similar fervor.

Today: I respond to the *Fire* in my heart.

You Who Question Souls

Leonard Cohen

Where have you been?
Do you remember who you are?
How can I assist you?
What led you to get lost?
Will you listen to my voice?
How did you forget your joy?
When will you let go?
Can you give yourself to love?
The questions you pose are endless.
And so is my soul's need for you.

Today: I listen for the question.

┼

Dweller in the Rainbow

Laurens van der Post

You dance amid the sky's colorful bow,
Flinging needed hope into the far realms,
A sign to each person in a desperate life
That their pain is not the ultimate end.
Anticipation of the lessening of troubles
Sings through the spectrum of colors
In which you dwell as a bringer of change.
You reside as a bright promise of better days,
Like the parting of dark clouds showing light
After a crushing storm with thrashing rain.

Today: I receive hope from the *Dweller in the Rainbow*.

Unspeaking Partner to My Sorrow

Rainer Maria Rilke

The gift of your tender presence
Companions me without words.
Your kindhearted love carefully rests
On the breast of my ashen sorrow.
Your compassion accompanies me
Like the soft assuredness of moonlight.
Your empathy touches my memories,
Easing painful remembrance of loss.
Your care soothes my aching heart
When it languishes in emptiness.

Today: I receive comfort from my *Unspeaking Partner*.

Beauty Ever Ancient, Ever New

St. Augustine

O Ancient Beauty, primordial love,
Seeded in the secret of every self.
You plant yourself permanently
As the mainstay of each one's life.
How frequently you reveal yourself
In unexpected form and manner,
Touching our hearts with quiet hope,
Stirring the embers of our faith,
Rousing us with your pure loveliness
As you visit our lives ever anew.

Today: I watch for how *Beauty* visits me.

---+---

Forgiver

John 8:10–11

When those who admit they have sinned
Come to you with contrite hearts,
Some easily accept your merciful welcome
While others question if it could be true.
As for myself I have sometimes wondered
If I take your forgiveness for granted,
If I go about my reckless, selfish ways
With assurance that you will absolve me.
How crucial to remember that imperative last line
I'd like to disregard: "Go now, *and sin no more.*"

Today: I relate to others as one who is forgiven.

Deep Well

Kathy Sherman

How far down into my secret self do I go?
How far until I find you whom I seek?
How often until I am saturated with love?
Further, always further, so it seems.
Lower the bucket of prayer into the depths.
Slowly bring it forth and taste its treasure.
This constant dipping inwardly to the Source
Can be a slow, tedious, and lengthy process.
At other times, the bucket falls without effort
And I draw forth quickly, drink until I am full.

Today: I draw forth from my *Deep Well*.

Bridegroom

Christopher Idle

You set your heart on my soul
And woo me into fuller relationship.
You stand at the altar of my life
In hope of a total commitment
To the faithful love you propose.
My heart see-saws in response.
Going toward. Returning back.
Hesitant to truly give you my all.
Thank you for patiently waiting
As I struggle with a complete "yes."

Today: I give my love to the *Bridegroom*.

Searcher of Hearts

Romans 8:27–28

Some believe you intensely look
For what is shabby and sinful
In the depths of our veiled selves.
Perhaps what you truly seek
Is our treasure of inner goodness,
That cache of love you infused
At the moment of our becoming.
Our inheritance of your goodness
Never truly dies. It only hides out
Until it's ready to be claimed.

Today: I allow more of my goodness to be found.

＋

The One Who Keeps Vigil With No Candle

Rainer Maria Rilke

As still as a silent, breathless dusk,
As calm as a dove settling into night,
You need no candle to vigil with us
Through the darkness of problems
And the grey months of heartache.
In days and years of extended illness
And in situations with no resolution,
You are an attentive eagle on her nest
Watching like a mother with her children,
Encouraging us to not fear the unseen.

Today: I vigil with the One who vigils with me.

Goddess

When I first heard you addressed
In this startling, fearful manner,
The word "pagan" spun in my mind.
Now this naming no longer distresses.
My view of your myriad attributes
Includes more than the masculine.
If you are "God," then "Goddess," too.
I envision you as queenly, motherly,
Wearing robes of threaded beauty,
Sitting within the realm of divinity.

Today: I reflect on feminine aspects of divinity.

Medicine of Dawn

Macrina Wiederkehr

Awakening from the slumbering night
I gratefully open my entire being to you,
Receiving spiritual medication for my life,
Vitamins of grace for my soul's journey.
Each morning as I enter into prayerfulness
I receive from your abundant medicine chest
Effective remedies for a lack of enthusiasm,
A renewed strength for the ability to love,
A clearer motivation for my daily occupation,
And an endless portion of healing grace.

Today: I remember to take my daily *Medicine*.

Labyrinth of Mystery

Harry Hagan

We are born into life's grey paradox
Of discovering our true home with you.
We locate a corner of your peace,
Then misplace it in the bustling world.
We find a focused direction for a while
But seem to lose it time and again.
We perpetuate this pattern of journeying
Until we eventually realize that you
Are wherever we are on the path of life,
No matter how labyrinthine it may be.

Today: I am at peace as I find my way.

The Pure One

The Qur'an

Trying to identify you as the Pure One
Presents a challenge from my culture.
For I have become too accustomed
To humankind's easy acts of pollution
Muddying the lucid waters of the heart.
I have experienced far too much
Of my own and others' deceitfulness.
I look to you with admiration and awe,
Trying to perceive your crystal clearness,
Amazingly free from all forms of falseness.

Today: I make an effort to be more transparent.

Unceasing Kindness

Like a caressing soft breeze
With a ceaseless whisper,
Or a gentle touch on the cheek
Whose imprint remains.
Like a compassionate gaze
Forever remembered,
Or a hand extended openly
Always ready to bestow.
So are you, Unceasing Kindness,
Ever present to our concerns.

Today: I bring *Kindness* with me.

July

In Islam we have two terms: *Tanzih* and *Tashbih*. *Tanzih* means that God is beyond any similarity to anything. God is the ultimate unknown, the ultimate unknowable, the great beyond, which we can't comprehend. That is the primary definition of God.

However having said that, we do need to know something about God. So God is identified by descriptive names or attributes. These could be called the adjectives of God, descriptive names like the compassionate, the merciful, the almighty, the powerful, the all-seeing. God does not have eyes, but he sees. God does not have ears, but he hears. The Koran even speaks of God's hand and God's face. These descriptions are used, but it is unanimously thought that they do not in any way describe an anthropomorphic view of God, but rather a theomorphic view of man. It is that which is being described.

—*Imam Feisal Abdul Rauf*

Creator of the Shimmering Sound

Neil Douglas-Klotz

Like a harp string gently plucked
Or the flickering whoosh of wings,
Like the swaying of sparkling grasses
And the sighing wind in the pines,
So is your sweet harmony in my soul.
Your glistening resonance awakens
And stirs me toward a timeless love,
Vibrating like an iridescent melody.
Delicate chords of divinity touch my life
Until all of it dances and shines with you.

Today: I resonate with the *shimmering sound*.

JULY 2

Wakan-Tanka

Native American

In past centuries when buffalo herds thrived
And land belonged to those who respected it,
Black Elk and his Lakota people invoked you,
Confident of your purpose in the universe.
This Great Plains tribe still calls out to you,
Their mysterious, great Spirit who gives life.
Each time they speak your precious name
They give voice to what is innately believed:
All beings are related in the sacred hoop of life.
All are brothers and sisters under the same sky.

Today: I look at the sky and remember all are one.

Fortress

Psalm 62:1–2

No high, walled-in city are you.
No bunkers or layers of concrete.
No tough steel girders of separation.
Your fortification is invisible,
A defense of courage and grace,
A formation of firm empowerment.
You are the One who protects us
From enemies within and without.
You are strength against addiction
And anything that strives to harm us.

Today: I am empowered by the *Fortress*.

Spirit of Justice

Mary Lou Kownacki

Your integrity is implanted in everyone
But set aside or lost in self-absorption.
Prejudice and ugly bias, disregarded.
The world's continued oppression, denied.
The indignity of the disabled, unnoticed.
The gap between rich and poor, ignored.
What will it take for the over-privileged
To hear your imploring voice of justice?
When will those with more than enough
Turn and give attention to those with less?

Today: I do something to act for *Justice*.

Ruler of My Heart

Tame the wildness in me
That wants to leap away
And do my own thing
Without regard for others.
Enliven the wildness in me
That gets overly complacent
With a too predictable life.
Rule over my flip-flop heart.
Do whatever it takes
To join the best in me with you.

Today: My heart listens to its *Ruler*.

Artist of the Universe

With one deft brush stroke
Something lovely emerges.
A world of boundless beauty,
One of symmetry, intricacy,
Simplicity, vitality, and unity.
The vast painting of creation
With its colorful, panoramic vista
Speaks wordlessly to our hearts
Of the dynamic, creative passion
Flowing from your imagination.

Today: I marvel at the *Artist*'s handiwork.

Divine Parent

Edward Hays

You carefully take us by the hand
And guide us on our way each day,
Watching over us diligently,
Nudging us on with encouragement.
You give us wings of freedom
While keeping us close to your heart.
You comfort us when we are hurt
And cheer us on when we succeed.
You correct us when we do wrong
And relish us always as your own.

Today: I place my hand in the *Divine Parent's* hand.

JULY 8

✝

The Physician

Kabir

Whether we want to admit it or not,
There's often some woundedness in us,
A concealed or deserted lesion of spirit
Begging for our undivided attention.
You are the supreme inner Physician,
Medicine for whatever ails our hearts,
A touch of regard for what we ignore,
A voice of love for recurring failure,
A healing aid for endless bruising,
A sure remedy for emotional misery.

Today: I bring what needs healing to the *Physician*.

The True Rest

Julian of Norwich

Rest for the frequently restless.
Rest for the easily slighted.
Rest for the unjustly treated.
Rest for the inwardly disturbed.
Rest for the innocently harmed.
Rest for the physically pained.
Rest for the harshly betrayed.
Draw us close when we are in need.
Do not let us forget what we can receive.

Today: I find needed rest in *The True Rest*.

Womb of Love

Edwina Gateley

Can I allow myself enough surrender
To be contained by you, Womb of Love?
Can I let myself be vulnerable with you,
To be at peace without self-performance?
Can I trust that you will hold me gently
And provide for nurturance of my soul?
Can I rest without any fearful concern
Of the why, the what, the how, of my life?
I can do all of this if I will remember
How you enfold me in your eternal care.

Today: I am held in the *Womb of Love*.

Fountain of Holiness

We do not throw in a useless coin
And make some kind of empty wish,
Or sit close to the gushing waters
And simply admire their loveliness.
You ask us to leap into the source,
To be thoroughly saturated.
We are to be absorbed by the cascade
And become one with your love.
As you flow through our being
We, too, become fountains of holiness.

Today: I absorb the *Fountain*'s flowing grace.

JULY 12

Bread of Life

John 6:35

You are the sustaining Bread of Life,
A ready provision of daily nutrition
Supplying for our spiritual growth.
You are food for generous service,
Sustenance for intimate union with you.
You come to us in various forms:
Eucharist and loving relationships,
In little and big touches of caring,
And in those subtle, inner stirrings
That enrich us with a deeper love of you.

Today: I am nourished by the *Bread of Life*.

Seed of Wholeness

Mary Ferring

Inside the core of each seed, no matter
How large or how tiny, a potential waits
For the life within to lift its face to the sun
And gift the world with a burst of freshness.
Such is your life within me, the potential
For wholeness, a seed of grace so vast
That each kernel of my latent goodness,
Whether it is unknown or undeveloped,
Can manifest its inherent greenness
And grow into a harvest of love.

Today: I attend to the *Seed of Wholeness* in me.

JULY 14

Awakener

Nan Merrill

Sometimes you are the Zen master
Bonking the sleeping meditator
With the hard stick of attentiveness,
Demanding immediate attention.
Sometimes you are the gentle parent
Come to rouse us from our sleep,
Tickling our knees and our toes,
Calling us into fuller consciousness.
Always you are the One who urges:
"Wake up! Observe! Pay Attention!"

Today: I am awake to what stirs in me.

Giver of Names

Laurens van der Post

To name is to be known by the designator.
And so it is with you, our Giver of Names.
We humans have boldly assigned a word
To every person and particle of existence.
Yet, this may well not be the true name
That rests on the breath of your knowing.
I wonder today what name you give me
As you lovingly peruse my journey of life.
What word or words do you call me
To express how you perceive my truest self?

Today: I ponder what the *Giver of Names* might call me.

Higher Power

Bill Wilson

How strongly I cling to control,
To insisting life will go my way,
Thinking it is all up to me,
That I can manage on my own.
I do not like to surrender,
To yield, to acquiesce to you,
To admit I am truly powerless
Without your strength and grace.
I wonder why I refuse to let go,
For you have so much to offer me.

Today: I surrender a bit more to my *Higher Power*.

Defender of Women and Children

Mary Kathleen Speegle Schmitt

War and poverty find their prey
Most often in women and children.
Through the ages it has been so
And still this reality exists today.
It is not surprising to consider you
As the Defender of the innocent,
As chief guardian of the powerless.
Your compassion flows into their tears.
Your heart knows their endless sorrow,
And wonders why we do not help them.

Today: I make an effort to support the defenseless.

The Quilter

Mary Ruth Broz, Barbara Flynn

How steady are your grace-full hands
As they tirelessly take the remnants
Of what we tend to discard as useless,
Creating a pattern of surprising unity.
You bring together these isolated events
Into a meaningful design of wholeness,
Finding amid our turmoil and struggle
Enough goodness to bind them together.
O Quilter of what we deem worthless,
Show us what we do not easily see.

Today: I look for the pattern of *The Quilter* in my life.

The One Who Calls

Y ou communicate with my secret self
And invite me to stretch beyond my fences,
To listen to what aches deep inside,
To face disruption and find growth there,
To accept the reality of imperfection,
To live deeper in the heart of the day,
To not lean on what others might think,
To accept affirmation without excusing,
To enter conflict with loving respect,
To grow deeper in union with your love.

Today: My secret self responds.

---†---

Distant One

Karl Rahner

Who has not had their moments
When you seemed unreachable?
Who has not known darkness
Thick enough to keep you hidden?
Who has not sought futilely
For a tangible sign of your presence?
Who has not waited patiently
For an answer that does not come?
When you are the Distant One,
That is when faith roots itself deeply.

Today: I reflect on how my faith is rooted.

Chief Cornerstone

Matthew 21:33–43

Like the first stone of a strong foundation
Linking together all the other stones,
You are the fundamental source of unity
Connecting and binding us with your love.
When anger and intolerance force us apart
We lose sight of the base of our oneness
And the loving linkage we have with you.
Remind us, when we separate ourselves
From one another by hostile argumentation,
To build our relationship upon your love.

Today: I am linked to others by the *Chief Cornerstone*.

Tear-Wiper

Ruth Marlene Fox

Shedding tears is neither a lack of faith
Nor a signal of personal weakness.
When afflictions too massive to contain
Push open the floodgates of our heart,
When tormenting hurts rise upward
And press teardrops from our eyes,
You do not reprimand or admonish us.
Instead, when we succumb to weeping
You reach to softly catch our teardrops
With the loving touch of your compassion.

Today: I am grateful for the *Tear-Wiper's* touch.

JULY 23

Illumined One

Hafiz

Illumined One, full of unfading light
Too copious to be kept to yourself.
A thousand stars do not compare,
A million moonbeams are no equal
To your illumination emitting in us.
If only we could see your radiance
When we encounter one another,
Perhaps greed, meanness, and envy
Would fall from our leaden hearts
Like hailstones leaving a burdened cloud.

Today: I see the *Illumined One* shining in all.

The Enricher

The Qur'an

Like soup without salt,
Like song without notes,
Like heart without love,
Like lily without scent,
Like sea without waves,
Like bird without wings,
Like flute without sound,
Like sorrow without tears,
So is my life without you
Who enrich each part of it.

Today: I notice how *The Enricher* gifts me.

Ocean of Joy

Kabir

Oh, that we could swim forever
In the sea of your unending joy.
Oh, that we might set happy sail
Upon the waters of your delight.
It's all close by, waiting for us
If only we stop our crazy pace
And allow our manacled calendars
To fall away from our tethered lives.
Now is the time, not later,
To let go and leap into your joy.

Today: I take the plunge.

Companion of My Solitude

Your presence makes the difference
Between aloneness and loneliness.
Your companionship quiets me.
A loving stillness encircles my being.
I can reside in my solitariness
And not grow restless or fearful.
Knowing you are here with me
Allows my spirit to be at peace,
To be alone without feeling isolated
Because you are ever by my side.

Today: I choose to have some time alone.

Eternal Truth

St. Augustine

In this world filled with half-truths,
Outright lies, and acceptable deception,
How extremely grateful I am for you.
You are the One whose heart is true,
The One who will never deceive.
But how can I have this certitude?
How can I be assured I know you?
Only by paying very close attention
To my motivations and desires,
Only by the daily working of integrity.

Today: *Eternal Truth* influences how I live.

$+$

Silent Potency

Neil Douglas-Klotz

You are ready at any moment
To stir and activate our potential,
To move our lethargy into action,
To change despair into hopefulness,
To soften love that has hardened,
To awaken slowly dying dreams,
To uplift spirits caught in sadness,
To guide the mind to clear thinking,
To strengthen wills that are weakened,
To free that which has been bound.

Today: *Silent Potency* moves in me.

---+---

Quencher of Thirst

Rabindranath Tagore

Come to us, Quencher of Thirst,
And relieve our endless yearning.
Come to the desert of our busyness
And refresh our parched attention.
Come to the arid land of boredom
And pour enthusiasm into our prayer.
Come to the wasteland of worry
And satisfy us with your stillness.
Come to the wilderness of denial
And fill us with growthful authenticity.

Today: I get in touch with my thirstiness.

┿

Luminous Web That Holds Everything in Place

Barbara Brown Taylor

You are like an exquisite spider web
With transparent dewdrops of dawn.
You sparkle like crystal in our hearts
Joining one wet bead with another.
Every part of the gossamer netting
Connects with you through the web.
Even though we feel apart from you
Or disengaged from one another,
We are the jeweled dewdrops of beauty
Joined as one with you, Luminous Web.

Today: I am joined to all in the *Luminous Web*.

The Realized

Beatrice Bruteau

There are those tiny slips of awareness
When, in the briefness of moments,
I glimpse and realize something of "you."
I comprehend with the totality of my being
The tenderness of your loving presence,
The wonder of your vast transcendence.
Then this graced recognition fades swiftly
And I am tempted to question if I imagined you.
All that is left to me is the delicious memory
Of how you opened the door.

Today: My memories of *The Realized* sustain me.

August

I used to be able to speak of "knowing" God or at least to imagine that there was some definable content to the word. Now, because it speaks of Mystery so vast and so deep that I cannot dare even to try to imagine it, that word GOD reduces me to silence. God beyond all names, God who seems to be everything at once, and yet, paradoxically, closer to nothing (no-thing) than to any thing. I used to wonder how I could "love" this God who so far surpasses anything I can imagine or name. Now I sense that when I respond to the cues that move me to expand my awareness and my love, it is that God who is the Source of Life in this creation who is doing the prodding. I sense that it is when I love the creation in as selfless and caring and compassionate a way as I can, when I am most reflecting in my human being the Self-giving of God's own nature, that is when I am loving God. Or perhaps I could say that then God is loving God's Self through me.

—*Elaine M. Prevallet, S.L.*

AUGUST 1

Earth Designer

Edward Hays

As vibrating particles of exploding stars
Gathered to form this exquisite planet
Your love stretched through each part
And urged it into astonishing beauty.
We approach with respect and gratitude
All the intricate parts of our dear Earth.
We enter into and partake of its life
With a careful touch of awed reverence.
Help us to look with wondrous eyes
As we behold the grandeur of your creation.

Today: I behold our planet with wide-open eyes.

AUGUST 2

Shakti

Hindu

How you twirl and spin as you move
With your creative empowerment
Through the strands and layers of life.
A feminine embodiment of divine energy,
In your womb of love you regenerate life.
You are the one who restores balance,
Preserving what carries creation onward,
Destroying what keeps new life from birthing.
In every moment you encourage change,
Insisting on transition as a part of transformation.

Today: I gain renewed strength to meet change.

Ground of Being

Paul Tillich

There is no tyranny in your divine essence.
Rather, you are part of the cause and effect
Of this intrinsic world and of our very self.
You, the solid base upon which all exists,
Remain beyond our greatest comprehension.
We can only speak about and proclaim you
Through the guiding help of symbol and story.
Still, we dare to approach and believe in you,
Because somewhere deep within our soul
We know you are who you are.

Today: I am rooted in the *Ground of Being*.

✝

Holy Memory

Evelyn Hunt

When you offered your self to your loved ones
You urged, "Do this in remembrance of me."
That sacred request took hold in their hearts
And carried itself down through the ages to us.
Since that moment we go on in our own lives
Remembering you not only in bread and wine
But in every action of ours done in honor of you.
Each time we take your teachings to heart
And focus on having them come to life in us
You resurrect as Holy Memory in our midst.

Today: I remember.

---✝---

Trusted Guide

Psalm 73:21–24

If only I would keep in mind
That you are there beside me
When I'm searching for a way,
Struggling with a decision,
Wondering about a response.
If only I would trust you
To inform my decisions,
To influence my insights,
To guard my heart's direction.
If only I would trust you.

Today: I renew my trust in the *Guide.*

✝

Strength of My Heart

Psalm 18:1

I rely on you, Strength of My Heart,
To fill the gaps of my inadequacies.
Strength for when I limp along weakly,
Unable to activate what is best in me.
Strength to turn toward those in need
When my heart is hollow, my mind shallow.
Strength to carry me through confusion,
To bolster my faith when it declines.
Strength for the times I am tempted
To turn from what facilitates my growth.

Today: I accept *Strength* where I am weak.

✝

Mother Bear

Hosea 13:8

Do you care for us that intensely?
Do you guard us that devotedly?
Is your protection of our sacred soul
Really as ferocious as a mother bear
Safeguarding her vulnerable little ones?
If this is as the prophet Hosea states
Then why do I not value more fully
The precious gift of your loyal love?
Growl in my life every once in awhile
So I remember your affection for me.

Today: I give thanks for *Mother Bear's* affection.

┼

Unifier

Nan Merrill

We need you, divine Unifier,
To join what has broken apart
in our human relationships.
Perceived wrongs separate.
Jealousies increase hostility.
Misuse of power divides.
Selfishness easily isolates.
Disloyalty dissolves trust.
Bring us closer to one another.
Unify us in your one great heart.

Today: I move closer to those I avoid.

AUGUST 9

The Seer of All

The Qur'an

If only we had your extensive vision
And could see beyond our small self.
There would be fewer antagonisms
And less desire to demand revenge.
Harsh judgments would be pulled back
And our meager mercy greatly expanded.
For you observe the deeper part of us,
Our silent motivations and expectations.
You focus on what unites, not divides.
You see how we are more alike than different.

Today: My eyes join those of *The Seer of All*.

Sovereign of
My Illumined Heart

Hafiz

You are the golden circle
Of illumination
Filling my heart with radiance.
You are the aura of light
Animating my innate goodness,
Shining through my poverty.
You reign supreme
In this resplendent site of love.
I give you my entire heart.
Please keep it well lit.

Today: My heart is illumined.

Root of Union

Kabir

Like thick, gnarled roots
Of an old cypress tree
Spreading beyond itself.
Like the extended roots
Of the communal aspen
birthing fresh saplings
From the original source.
So is our union with you
Held strongly by your love.
Deep and wide is our connection.

Today: I am rooted in love.

---+---

Provider

Psalm 103:1–5

When my spirit is pressed and harried,
You provide space for slowing down.
When my body is weary and worn,
You provide rest and rejuvenation.
When my emotions overwhelm me,
You provide balancing perspective.
When my mind fills with criticism,
You provide teachings on nonjudgment.
When my heart sags with defeat,
You provide needed sources of support.

Today: I accept gratefully what is provided.

Near One

Karl Rahner

Can it really be possible
We are so tightly bonded
That our breath is one breath?
Can it be you are intertwined
In every thought of mine
That steps into consciousness?
Can it be that your great love
Forever mingles with my own?
If so, I gladly lose myself
In the closeness of your presence.

Today: The *Near One* breathes with me.

The Trustee

The Qur'an

All I am and all I have
Is in your safe-keeping.
You oversee my deep self
With its treasure of goodness.
At any moment in time
I can approach you
And withdraw from this bounty.
You supervise these gifts
And encourage me to use them
For the benefit of others.

Today: *The Trustee* draws forth a gift of mine.

Wordless Action

Neil Douglas-Klotz

We call upon you,
Cry out your name,
Beg for assistance,
Pray for relief.
We hear and see nothing,
Think you eternally distant,
Inattentive to our need.
Yet, all the while we pray
You are acting on our behalf,
Quietly taking care of us.

Today: I am comfortable with silent communication.

The Poet

Rabindranath Tagore

Like a poet gathering words
Into the most succinct of verses,
You bring together the pieces
Of my often fragmented life,
Inviting me to read within it
What I rarely behold or understand.
For there lies the deeper meaning
Of my journey's hills and valleys,
The story of your faithful love
Written on every line of my life.

Today: *The Poet* writes love songs on my heart.

Mediator

When we live out of our weakness
You intervene with your grace
And draw us back toward you.
When we fail to live as you desire,
You negotiate our turning 'round
And coming home to your love.
When we step aside from our principles,
You urge us to return to what is true.
You never give up on our inborn ability
To live the best of who we truly are.

Today: I move toward what is good.

The One Who Does Not Pass Away

Dorothee Soelle

All those useless queries of mine
When a dear one departs this life,
My wondering about the "where,"
The "perhaps," the "if," and the "how"
Of their now disembodied existence.
All these unanswerable questions
I hand over into the mystery of yourself,
The One Who Does Not Pass Away.
Take these endless wonderings of mine.
Tuck them into your eternally alive heart.

Today: I let go and let be what is unanswerable.

Heart of Mercy

Ephesians 2:4–5

You are rich in mercy and kindness.
No matter the skin color or creed,
The wealthiest or the poorest,
The most pure or most tainted,
The weakest or the strongest,
You extend your forgiveness
And continual understanding.
Anyone is a potential candidate
For receiving your copious mercy
When they turn their heart toward you.

Today: I, too, will show mercy.

---+|---

Sacred Essence

Edward Hays

If we could realize
The beauty of your being,
Every particle of us
Would bend the knee
And cry out, "Holy!"
Our worries and woes
Would fall aside,
Dissolve in amazement
At the discovery
Of your essence everywhere.

Today: I bend the knee of my heart to *Sacred Essence*.

My Cup

Psalm 16:5

You are the container of our love,
The One with endless affection
Pouring generously into our lives.
You are the container of our hope,
The One who holds our possibilities,
Giving us reason to live fully.
You are the container of our faith,
The One who encloses our confidence,
Lessening our fears and anxieties.
You, the Cup, contain all we need.

Today: Each container I use reminds me of *My Cup.*

✝

The Clement

The Qur'an

Softness suffuses your presence
But never weakens your strength.
Leniency shapes your mercy
Yet does not lessen your justice.
Compassion marks your judgment
Without detracting from the truth.
For you are The Clement One,
The calm current of loving divinity,
Gently accompanying each of us
When we sink into our weakness.

Today: My approach to others is gentle.

Ageless One

No worries about getting old.
No concern about new wrinkles.
No attention to weight gain or loss.
None of that human distress
That preoccupies our egoic lives.
You are the Ageless One,
Wafting lightly through the eons
With one thing on your mind:
Love, love, love, love, love, love,
And how to assist us in living it.

Today: I pay attention to love rather than to aging.

Soft Light of the Waning Sun

Macrina Wiederkehr

Dusk slips its easy cover over the day
And quietly invites life to slow down.
Darkness slowly gathers the sunlight
And tucks it away smoothly until dawn.
Birds bend their heads under soft wings
And day's bright energy bows to stillness.
Such is your gentle approach with us.
At certain times you move us into a quiet
That includes darkness in place of light.
Let us not fear when the night comes upon us.

Today: I slow down and ease into stillness.

Door

John 10:7

You are the Door to love,
To freedom, to belonging.
You are the Door to change,
To growth, to wholeness.
You greet us, arms wide open,
Welcoming us with joy.
You invite us to step inside,
To trust what awaits us
When we accept your invitation
To be all that we can be.

Today: I accept the invitation.

Knower of My Emptiness

Rainer Maria Rilke

I can easily hide out
From everyone but you.
I can pretend fullness
But you won't be fooled.
You observe the emptiness
In my sepulchered spirit.
You try to convince me
That being emptied of ego
Is the prerequisite
For being filled with love.

Today: I befriend *My Emptiness*.

Potter

Jeremiah 18:1–6

Each of us at the time of our birthing
Came forth as soft clay in your hands,
Unresisting to your graced movement,
Easily giving ourselves to your ways.
What happens to us as we grow older?
When does our spirit lose that softness?
How does our mind become unyielding,
Unbendable, resistive, and rigid?
Soften what has become hardened in us.
Restore our ability to bend to your love.

Today: The *Potter* finds my heart pliable.

Friend of Children

Anselm Grün

You would be the last one
To snarl about a crying child
During a dignified church service.
You would be the first one
To welcome a waiting unborn
Known to have disabling features.
You would be the only one
To see deeply in a child's soul
The utter purity and radiant light
That shines on the face of angels.

Today: I resolve to be kind to every child.

✝

Beloved Eternity

St. Augustine

Always you wait for us beyond here.
No pushing, shoving, or hurrying.
Simply waiting with arms wide open,
Encouraging us to value present life,
To give ourselves fully to its process,
But not to seize it too tightly.
In death, the love we experience here
Will be gathered into a rainbow of oneness
As we are carried peacefully home to you,
Our Beloved Eternity, our Forever Love.

Today: I engage my life fully, yet hold it lightly.

$$\dagger$$

Bestower of Fruitfulness

Ephesians 3:20

Through my years of accomplishment
I have learned that all human success
Originates from the source of your grace.
Any good that I may possibly undertake,
Each talent that I am able to use well,
Every extended act of charity I carry out,
All this fruitfulness is bestowed by you.
It is your power working through me
Ripening my innate capacities for good
That does "more than I can ask or imagine."

Today: I am empowered by the *Bestower of Fruitfulness.*

Rock of Safety

Psalm 31:2

Like a boulder thick and sturdy,
You constantly stabilize my self,
Offering a solid grounding place
So I do not fall away from you.
When I find myself distracted
By elements of my false self
You are a steadfast foundation,
A strong, protective constancy,
The One who bids me come
And stand upon the truth again.

Today: I find my stability in the *Rock of Safety*.

September

In India we find the same idea accepted which is expressed at the beginning of the Fourth Gospel, that God and (God's) name are one. In Vedanta, God's name is called the mantra. There are various mantras, depending on the particular aspect of God a devotee chooses to worship. The teacher gives his disciple the mantra at the ceremony of initiation, and enjoins on him to keep it sacred and to meditate upon the aspect of God which it represents for the rest of his life. The essence of the disciple's Chosen Ideal is concentrated in the mantra in the form of a sound-symbol. As the name of God is repeated, the spiritual power with which it is charged becomes evident. By hallowing the name over and over again, we let God take possession of our conscious minds so that finally, no matter what we are doing or saying or thinking, some part of our minds will be praising (God).

—*Swami Prabhavananda*

SEPTEMBER 1

Divine Magnet

Edward Hays

Draw me toward your love.
Attract me to what really counts.
Pull me away from distractions
That keep my heart unfocused.
Let there be a strong connection
Between your presence and mine,
So that in each aspect of life
I stay closely in touch with you.
Captivate my heart so completely
That I continually return to you.

Today: The *Divine Magnet* draws me to love.

Word of Mercy

Bernadette Farrell

Your words of mercy echo in my spirit:
"I forgive you for what you have done."
"You can start over. Begin again."
"I'll be there as you recover."
"Trust that there's a better way."
"Try your best to not do that again."
"I know you can change your ways."
May I also speak your words of mercy
In my response to those who stray,
Fail and fall, and attempt to start over.

Today: The words I speak contain *Mercy*.

Ultimate Guru

Dilgo Khyentse

Will I let you be my Ultimate Guru?
Am I willing to learn from you?
Am I ready to entrust my entire self
Into your wisdom and guidance?
Am I able to do the hard work
Of following your essential teachings?
Am I vulnerable and courageous
To do what turns out to be difficult?
Am I free enough to let go
Of what keeps me from growing?

Today: I give myself to the *Ultimate Guru*.

Irresistible Beauty

Wisdom 7:29

You have overpowered my heart
In moments of unsuspecting prayer
By slipping into my fat distractions
And quietly closing my mind-door.
You have abruptly stunned me
In those moments with creation
When a look, a sound, a touch
Of the ordinariness before me
Breathed its adoration of you.
How blessed I am, how blessed.

Today: I find you in the ordinary beauty I behold.

The Old One

Albert Einstein

In times past many pictured you
As some ancient, bearded geezer
Looking in on the world from afar.
But now we value your nearness,
You, The Old One from foreverland.
You teach us while we sit near you
In the rocking chair of your wisdom.
We listen intently to how it was long ago
When your eternal peace and integrity
Were the only things the world knew.

Today: *The Old One* teaches me.

Reality

Rabbi Rami Shapiro

When all else fails to give me assurance
And developed opinions sit smugly
In the endless river of my rolling mind,
I come to this simple, basic name for you,
Stripped of emotional and intentional bias,
Emptied of hidden pretentiousness.
This title speaks to me of a certainty
With no need of profound theories.
I can give my continual stream of opinions
Into your care and leave them there with you.

Today: I let my opinions rest.

The Weaver

Julia Esquivel

I am the loom full of promise.
You are the divine Weaver.
The colorful threads you merge
Consist of my life's components.
I do not see your interlacing
But I sense a steady movement
As the cloth of love develops.
I trust in what you are creating
As the shuttle of your action
Lifts in and out of my loomed self.

Today: The pieces of my day form a pattern of love.

SEPTEMBER 8

Surprise

David Steindl-Rast

Just about the time I get dogmatic,
Certain that I know it all,
You upend what I thought was fact.
Just about the time I drown in tears,
You enter in with unmitigated joy.
Just about the time I yawn in monotony
You come dancing in with a lively step.
Just about the time I think I know you,
You turn up, show another side of yours,
And there I am, surprised again.

Today: I am attentive to my inner stirrings.

SEPTEMBER 9

The Preserver

The Qur'an

You keep my love safely inside yours
Although mine tries to jump out.
You continue close contact with me
Even when I tend to ignore you.
You safeguard our relationship
Although I grow careless about it.
You sustain my desire to grow
When I turn my attention elsewhere.
You preserve my inner core of goodness
And never let me stray too far from it.

Today: I am well-preserved.

---✝---

Our Life

John 5:39–40

As essential as the body's heartbeat
Is for maintaining our life and health,
So are you vital to our every moment.
A steady rhythm of enduring love
Moving through our days and nights.
A constant source of life-giving presence
Sourcing and enriching our inner life.
Most of us disregard our heart's pattern
Just as we ignore how life-giving you are.
Wake us up to what we take for granted.

Today: My heartbeat reminds me of *Our Life*.

SEPTEMBER 11

Tender One

Like a parent cradling a distressed child,
A friend embracing the hurt of another,
A lover softly enfolding the other with care,
So you, Tender One, take us to your heart.
Your gentleness lessens our distress.
Your sympathetic care relieves our sorrow.
Your easy way of touching us with kindness
Diminishes what tries to overpower us.
Your tenderheartedness reaches far
And reminds us we are never totally alone.

Today: I remember the *Tender One* is with me.

Divine Seamstress

Mary Kathleen Speegle Schmitt

You sew together the fabric
Of our transformation.
You design the beautiful virtues
That clothe our soul.
You mend what we have torn
In our carelessness.
You thread your faithful love
Into our relationships.
You tailor our daily endeavors
With details of your goodness.

Today: I take my sewing to the *Divine Seamstress.*

Krishna

Hindu

As you joyfully play your flute,
You invite us to join with you
In embracing the dance of life.
As you direct us inwardly,
You invite us to inner truth.
As you eliminate what is false,
You invite us to become true love.
As you play your gleeful tricks,
You invite us to lighten up.
May we embody joy as you do.

Today: I embrace the dance of life with joy.

---✝---

Mother of Mystery

Edward Hays

When life does not readily supply
What I anticipate or think I need,
When the response of others
Fails to meet my expectations,
When the peaceful world I long for
Remains caught in self-destruction,
Take me into your welcoming arms
And teach me again about mystery.
Remind me to place in your care
What I cannot manage or change.

Today: The *Mother of Mystery* holds my concerns.

Companion of the Sorrowing

When our heart aches from loss
And our mind seems to be adrift,
When loneliness engulfs our grieving
With the fragile remnants of memory,
It can be helpful for us to remember
We do not weep alone in our sorrow.
You hold us in your gentle embrace,
Comforting us with murmurs of love.
Your compassionate, caring presence
Gives us courage and hope to go on.

Today: My *Companion's* heart holds my hurts.

---†---

Story Teller

You never stop teaching us
Through the story of our lives
And the heritage of our world.
You continually invite us closer,
To sit on the lap of your love,
To hear your compelling narratives
And learn of our divine inheritance.
In these ageless stories we listen to
The challenging human adventure
And discover how to find our way home.

Today: I listen to the *Story Teller*.

My Shield

Psalm 119:114

You defend me vigorously
From my strong enemies
And that includes myself,
Those brooding parts of me
That come charging fiercely
With weapons of aggression.
You are my strong defense
Against what tries to lure me
Away from your loving heart,
Away from my genuine self.

Today: *My Shield* protects me from harm.

✝

Hiding Place

Psalm 32:7

Ah, there are those days
When the best place to be
Is hiding out with you
Where stillness is to be found
And perspective from problems.
Where hope can be restored
And peace re-enters the mind.
Where joy waits to be savored
And mourning given her due.
Thank you for being my Hiding Place.

Today: I go to my *Hiding Place*.

The More

Barbara Brown Taylor

You are more than I expect,
More than I can handle.
You are more than I deserve,
More than I can ever earn.
You are more than my plenty,
More than I can wholly contain.
You are more than I believe,
More than I can comprehend.
Each day I receive more of you
As you add to my abundance.

Today: The *More* I receive, the more grateful I am.

---†---

Exceeding Joy

Our appreciation of you expands
With the gift of you in our rejoicings:
In the big occasions of celebration,
In the true happiness we have known,
In the mirth, delight, and pleasure,
The hilarity, cheer, and triumphs,
In the chuckles and sighs of delight,
The satisfied breath of contentment,
In the experience of awesome bliss,
And the "could dance forever" feelings.

Today: *Exceeding Joy* lives in my joy.

El Shaddai

Jewish

El Shaddai, God of the mountains,
The strong, noble, powerful one,
Whom Abraham and Sarah
Called by name in their prayer.
You are also "the breasted one"
Spoken to by prayerful ancients.
I call upon you, too, in my need,
To empower me in my uncertainty,
To embolden me in my fearfulness,
To strengthen me in my weakness.

Today: I look to *El Shaddai* for my strength.

Badge of Valor

John Micallef

Who wears you on their heart?
Every parent giving their utmost.
Those who counsel the addicted.
Police, firefighters, peacekeepers,
And emergency medical teams.
Teachers intent on helping students.
Nurses working exhausting shifts.
Volunteers who gladly lend their help
And all persons going beyond self
To touch another person with kindness.

Today: I join in giving of myself to others in need.

SEPTEMBER 23

One Who Brings Us Home

Mary Kathleen Speegle Schmitt

You are like those long night trips
When my parents brought me home
After an evening away visiting friends.
I fell fast asleep in the car's backseat
And when we finally made our arrival
One of them carried me quietly to bed.
So it is with You Who Brings Us Home.
When we entrust ourselves to your love,
You carry us quietly in your loving arms,
Bringing us back to where we belong.

Today: I entrust myself to the *One Who Brings Us Home*.

Supporter

Psalm 46:1–3

When things do not go as we wish,
When love falls out of our heart,
When disaster plummets our spirit,
When failure squelches our hope,
When betrayal destroys our trust,
When death snatches our joy,
When goodbye outweighs hello,
When confusion alters our vision,
When what we knew no longer exists,
You stand by us as our strong support.

Today: I can count on my *Supporter*.

---†---

Morning Song of Love

Macrina Wiederkehr

You awaken me at the break of day
With the melody of your love song
Strumming across my sleepy mind.
You call me to be in tune with you,
To arise with deep remembrance
Of the sweet harmony of your music.
Let me move into full wakefulness,
Attentive to your song within me
As I prepare to greet each morning.
Sing your love in me throughout the day.

Today: I hear the *Morning Song of Love* in me.

Great Illegal Immigrant

Edwina Gateley

You have "been there, done that."
Experienced rejection and alienation.
Been shoved aside, warned of reckonings.
Asked cruel questions, endured isolation.
When you stood before arrogant authorities
You, too, lacked any cultural credibility
And found few to come to your defense.
Your Spirit still travels among foreigners,
Still compassionates the unwanted,
Still urges us to give them a welcome.

Today: I will open my mind and heart a little wider.

Quiet of the Heart

Edward Hays

Quiet of the Heart, you are
Calm as a falling feather,
Serene as dusk's fading light,
Tranquil as the opening rose,
Restful as a cooing dove,
Gentle as the softening rain,
Hushed as a sleeping babe,
Peaceful as a blade of grass.
When I cease my foolish pace
I enter your undisturbed stillness.

Today: *Quiet* is in my heart.

Lover of Life

When we take that final breath
That wings us into eternity,
Will we be satisfied with life
And how we moved within it?
Will we have lived it fervently
Like you, Lover of Life?
Will we have savored existence
With eager and satisfying awareness?
Heard life's majestic rhythm
And discovered love inside it?

Today: The *Lover of Life* enhances my alertness.

Meaning of My Existence

Karl Rahner

For many years in my journey of life
I have searched for a deeper meaning,
One that gives purpose and direction.
I have learned that in every experience
And in each person who comes my way,
In theologies, philosophies, psychologies,
And every form of spirituality and prayer,
I find another pebble of truth on the path.
All lead me to discover who I am and why:
To enter into the fullness of union with you.

Today: I renew my desire to be in union with the divine.

The Reliever

The Qur'an

Alleviate what bothers me
About certain aspects of my life.
Lighten the burdens I carry
In my concern for others' woe.
Allay my fear of the future
And what it might bring to me.
Smooth the rough edges
That irritate my reckless mind.
Reduce the tension of my troubles
As I place greater trust in you.

Today: I seek relief from my burdens.

October

When I say that one can meet God immediately in your time too, just like in mine, I mean really God, the God past all grasp, the mystery beyond speech, the darkness that is light only to those who let themselves be swallowed by it unconditionally, the God who is now beyond all names. But equally it was just this God, no other, that I experienced as the God who descends to us, who comes near to us, in whose incomprehensible fire we do not in fact burn up, but rather come to be for the first time, and are eternally affirmed. The God beyond speech speaks [God's] self to us; in this speaking of [God's] unspeakableness we come to be, we live, we are loved, we are affirmed. . . .

—*Karl Rahner*

Listener

Your ear, beloved Listener, opened wide,
Pressed to each portion of my heart, my life.
Attuned to the slightest vibration of my being,
Attentive to the constant rhythms of my soul.
You hear the cry in the throat of my heart.
My troubles do not cease with your awareness
But they soften, loosen some of their grip,
Become bearable, touchable, endurable.
If your attentive solicitude blesses so fully,
Surely I, too, can listen that closely to others.

Today: I listen to others as the *Listener* does to me.

True Love

St. Augustine

In spite of our unfaithfulness,
You continue to be a reliable constant,
An unwavering, undying love.
Whether in good times or in bad,
We turn to you and you are there for us.
We show forth our best or our worst
And you continue to believe in us.
We wander askew or remain aloof
And you still leave the porch light on.
Because you are our one True Love.

Today: I join my heart to *True Love*.

Stream of Enduring Love

Here I am in my small, aging dinghy
Filled with the content of my life,
Moving on the current of your love.
Sometimes I want to get out of the boat,
Doubtful of where I might be going.
Once in a while, I feel the easy flow,
Allow the direction to carry me,
And rest without a care or concern.
These moments are when I glide best,
When the movement of you and I are one.

Today: I glide easily in the *Stream of Enduring Love*.

Safety Net

When I leave one situation for another
I take a risk and swing precariously
On the trapeze of my changing life,
Flying cautiously among the in-between.
How glad I am for your assured presence
As I let go of what has given me security.
When I do not find firm footage anywhere
You promise to catch me if I should fall.
Knowing this I can take those scary leaps
That fly me into the unknown future.

Today: I take a little leap toward growth.

Blessed Silence

Edward Hays

Lead me to you, Blessed Silence.
Take me to the zenith of stillness
Where even my quiet breathing
Sounds a bit noisy to me.
Shatter my fright of what I'll not hear
When there is nothing left to hear.
Gather all my lame, worn-out excuses
For why I must have endless words
In order to draw closer to you.
Do not speak to me. Just *be* with me.

Today: I am not afraid of *Blessed Silence*.

Harvest of My Heart

Edward Hays

When I pause to happily gather
The produce of my inner garden
Everything that yields abundance
Holds your flavor, scent, and shape.
The recognized fruits of daily effort,
The results of faithful discipline,
The increasing growth of healthy habits,
And the tender ripening of virtues,
All this comes from your grace,
From you, Harvest of My Heart.

Today: I collect my inner harvest with gratitude.

Caregiver of the Night

Macrina Wiederkehr

Night, with its unpredictable airs
And its ability to cast dark shadows
Need not frighten or dismay us.
Nothing that lurks in our unconscious
Or scurries about in our anxieties
Can contend with your love for us.
Whether we toss and turn wide-eyed
With restless worry or painful illness,
Or slumber with effortless contentment,
You cradle us with your safekeeping love.

Today: I am safe with the *Caregiver of the Night*.

---+---

Haunter of All That Is

Peter Steele, O.S.M.

Like an ethereal presence
You hang out everywhere.
Not a naughty or scary goblin,
Rather, an inquisitive observer,
A concerned, caring custodian,
Visiting every niche and closet
Where we stuff the undesired
Of our messy, blemished lives.
You haunt territories we ignore,
Hoping we will find you there.

Today: I visit one of my unwanted aspects of life.

Father

Luke 11:1–4

"Our Father" we say in prayer,
Perhaps not comprehending
The fullness of this greeting.
We come to you, true parent,
With assurance of your care.
The safe One whom we trust
To be an indispensable support.
The Father who knows our need
And who generously provides
For every nibble of daily bread.

Today: I pray "Our Father" with awareness.

Protector

Psalm 12:7

How much I need your defense
From my ego's insistent entitlement,
And pride that feeds on others' approval
Like free potato chips in a supermarket.
Sometimes I need you to guard me
From the mind's ruthless criticism
Of my failed attempts at growth.
You are a vigilant, faithful protector.
You have my best interests at heart.
Will I accept it when you come to my aid?

Today: I accept the *Protector's* advice.

Great Companion

Rufus Jones

In those wobbly moments of doubt
When useless fear invades ferociously,
In those extended heart-pilgrimages
Of searching and sobering discontent,
In those patterns of old behavior
That refuse efforts to be shaken off,
In those troubling, hurtful relationships
And ongoing disillusionments of life,
We have you with us, Great Companion,
To assure us that we do not travel alone.

Today: I can count on my *Great Companion*.

---†---

Guardian of the Grieving

You do much more than stand there
Being attentive to heart-sore spirits.
You lovingly embrace and closely guard
Those who feel bereft and lonely.
You vigilantly attend to each one
Lest they be overtaken by their sadness.
Your protective gaze of compassion
Softens the blows of their sorrow.
Guardian of those who have lost much,
Watch devotedly over those who mourn.

Today: I bring sorrowful ones to the *Guardian*.

Lady of the Seasons

Celtic

Song of the land, Paean of the sun,
Music of the sea, Dance of the air,
You gift us in swift passages of time
With memorandums of your love:
Your fruitful breath in summer,
Your graced stillness in winter,
Your hopeful resonance in springtime,
Your mellow contentment in autumn.
When we pause in conscious awareness
Each carries your messages to our spirit.

Today: I listen to the *Lady of the Seasons*.

Infinite Majesty

Job 37:1–5

Am I too independent to bow to you,
To admit to your sovereignty
Over my heart, over my entire life?
Am I too proud to acknowledge
Your ultimate powerfulness?
Am I too ignorant to recognize
Your authority in the cosmos?
Am I too blind to see your grandeur
Etched in the landscape of creation?
If so, shake loose my arrogance.

Today: I bow to *Infinite Majesty*.

Almsgiver

Psalm 36:7–9

Along with countless other beggars
Who rely on you for spiritual food,
I come with my own unfilled bowl,
Confident that I will surely receive
From the bounty of your goodness.
You know my poverty and give freely,
Enough to satisfy my spiritual hunger,
Plenty to nourish my famished soul.
No need to demand or be gluttonous
For I can be satisfied with what I obtain.

Today: I come with my begging bowl.

Coach in the Cave

Our sojourn of inner growth sometimes
Confines us to the cave's empty gloom.
In this silent, gray space of waiting
When we are unsure of how to proceed
We hear your voice of wisdom urging us:
"Do not be afraid, I am with you."
"Learn to love the silence."
"Trust this time of slow gestation."
"This is not a waste of your time."
"Breathe. Be at peace. Easy does it."

Today: I trust my *Coach in the Cave*.

✝

Forest That Always Surrounds Us

Rainer Maria Rilke

Trees know how to reckon with the seasons.
Giant sequoias stand tall with protection.
Evergreens offer homes to small creatures.
Pines suffuse a scent of ready welcome.
Great oaks endure dry summers, harsh winters.
Aspens huddle in their kindred community.
Your tranquil presence is like a quiet forest
Where we experience transforming calmness,
Leaning undisturbed on your abiding presence,
Reveling in the unspoken sense of peacefulness.

Today: I find peace in the *Forest That Always Surrounds Us*.

Home of My Loneliness

Karl Rahner

In the curve of my heart lies a hollow place
Where grudging loneliness asks a welcome.
In that empty chamber of solitariness
You rest your consistent, welcoming love
On the heartsick and patterned discontent
Of my gloomy days and shredded dreams.
You care for my loneliness with affection
During the times when no one and no thing
Soothes the deep yearning sitting listlessly
Inside the arid space of my discontented self.

Today: The *Home of My Loneliness* welcomes me.

She Who Is

Elizabeth Johnson

Finally you are being acknowledged,
Not as He Who Is but She Who Is.
Another face of divinity to guide us,
A feminine movement of aliveness,
A divine, relational, knowable presence.
You draw us into sacred community
And challenge troubling exclusivity
With your invitation of partnership.
You choose to reveal yourself to us
Through silent, intuitive glimpses.

Today: *She Who Is* invites me inward.

My Journey's End

Karl Rahner

No one knows the precise instant
When death steals their last breath,
When the heart that beats steadily
Ceases its rhythmic functioning.
Whenever this moment arrives,
You will be ready to welcome us,
Your faithful love sweeping us away
Into another sphere of existence.
Your radiance intertwined with ours
Assuring us there is no need to fear.

Today: I place hope in *My Journey's End*.

Spinning Woman God

Alla Renée Bozarth

You sit, spinning at the loom of life.
Your deep-creased, contented smile
Blessing each creative movement
As you fashion the fabric of existence.
You stretch out long rainbow threads
Throughout varied layers of the universe.
Fibers of clouds, skies, and sailing planets,
Black holes and strands of silvery starlight,
All come alive at your ancient touch
As you spin the royal pattern of your love.

Today: I spin a pattern of love into the day.

Principle

Mary Baker Eddy

If I shed every belief I have
And stood naked
In the nothingness of my knowing,
What would I have left?
Only you. Only you. Only you.
The entirety of my being
Would find its feeble feet
On the solid ground
Of your endless love,
The true nature that upholds me.

Today: I reflect on what grounds my love.

Comforting Darkness

Macrina Wiederkehr

You are my Comforting Darkness
When I need a silent place inside
To shield me from my ego's glare.
You are my Comforting Darkness
When I sit on a summer's night
Kissing the stars with my eyes.
You are my Comforting Darkness
When the shade of your compassion
Brings relief to the wilderness of grief
Pressing on my mournful heart.

Today: I draw nearer to *Comforting Darkness*.

Winged One

Exodus 19:3–5

O you with sky-spacious, eagled wings,
I ride confidently on your supportive love.
There I find the freedom for transformation.
Soaring on wisdoms of your liberating spirit
I let go of clinging to worn-out complaints.
Sail me further on your wide, expansive wings.
Take me to my interior place of honesty
To meet the parts of self that need changing.
Fly me though the murky clouds of resistance
Into the opening skies of your everlasting light.

Today: I sail on the wings of divine love.

Guardian of Death

Why is it necessary for you to guard death?
What could possibly damage or harm it?
Ah, but this is not about physical endings.
This death is of the sort that helps us live:
Unwanted closures that widen our mind,
Unsought changes that expand our heart.
These deaths rob us of our grasped treasures
And free us to move beyond our limited selves.
You guard these times of loss and letting go,
Knowing we need them if we are to grow.

Today: I accept my life's unwanted changes.

Gracious Gift

Your giving teaches me how to give.
No begrudging of your kind bestowals
That shape who I am and what I have.
No holding back from your generosity
Or any anxiety about depleted abundance.
No discontinuing your free offerings
Even when I forget to give you thanks.
No asking that I return similar favors
That I've received without requesting.
When will my giving begin to look like yours?

Today: I give without expecting in return.

—————————— ┼ ——————————

Voice in the Fog

Lost in thick layers of gloominess
I call out, "Where are you?"
"I'm here," you whisper back
As I strain to hear your voice.
"Are you really here?" I echo.
"Trust me," comes the response.
"But I can't see," I complain.
"Why do you need to see?"
You reply through the heavy fog,
"Is it not enough that I am here?"

Today: I listen to the *Voice in the Fog*.

Refuge from the Storm

Psalm 57:1

I found needed shelter from harm
The day of the violent hailstorm
When I hurriedly sought shelter
Under the wide sycamore branches.
That stormy day reminds me of you,
The One whose canopied refuge
Spreads an eternal awning of love.
When I feel tempestuous strife
I hurry in prayer to your safe haven
And my wild storms inside do no damage.

Today: The wide branches of *Refuge* shelter me.

The Witness

The Qur'an

You stand beyond, yet near, on life's periphery,
A faithful Witness to what stirs inside of me.
You attest to my attempts to change my ways
And observe how life events slowly empty me.
You know how I strive for clarity of purpose
And that I long to be a true friend of yours.
As the spiral of my spiritual growth spins
You behold the true intentions of my heart.
Should I ever need you to do so,
I know you would speak out on my behalf.

Today: I am honest with *The Witness*.

My Vision

Mary E. Byrne

Come, be the eyes of my spirit.
Set yourself firmly in my mind.
Regulate the abode of my heart.
Influence the regions of my will.
Let nothing be as influential
For my daily comings and goings
As your vision leading me onward.
Let me see with new eyes
So that your perception motivates
All I am and all I do.

Today: My Vision influences my attitudes.

———————— ┼ ————————

Delight of All the Saints

Litany of the Sacred Heart

Your wide heart of exquisite acceptance
Holds a special fondness for the saints.
You gather them into your assembly
Whether they are grumpy or glad.
You hold them close to your merciful love
In spite of any history of wrongdoing.
You welcome them in their conversions
And assist them in their ways of service.
We are your little saints in the making
In whom you also take great delight.

Today: The *Holy One* delights in me.

November

By naming God everything that makes God God, we come daily to see God differently, to see God wholly. More than that, by naming God the sum total of created goodness, we come to see the rest of life differently as well. In the first place, we see God present to every distinct moment, every separate segment of life. In the second place, we come to see every distinct moment of life, every gracious mortal being around us charged with that presence. We come to see that every facet of life—all of them, each of them—as glints of the Divine. We get a fuller picture of God. At the same time, we get a deeper understanding of the sacredness of a creation that shares in this divinity.

When we name God fully, all of life becomes an exercise in contemplation. We touch the divine dimensions of ourselves. We see God everywhere. We feel divinity everywhere. We recognize God everywhere. And, eventually, we become what we think about. We become what we see, make holy what we touch, make sacred what we are.

In this tradition, no single name names God. . . . Clearly, if God is really God, no one name can possibly hold all the allusions, say all the concepts, breathe in one breath all the qualities that are God. That awareness changes the way we see both God and life.

—*Joan Chittister*

God of Our Ancestors

Daniel 2:23

A long ancestral line of women and men
Proceed ahead of us on our journey,
Leaving vivid traces of their history.
They mark the path with their wisdom,
Fill the air with fragrant goodness
And smile with jubilant satisfaction.
You are at the head of this long line
With innumerable people of good will.
Your light spreads throughout all of them,
A great love flowing from them to us.

Today: I embody one virtue of my ancestors.

---+---

Vigilant One

Luke 22:39–46

You vigiled those frightening hours alone
In the Garden while friends slept nearby.
You know what it is like to face the future
Wondering if you have courage to do it.
You watch now with us in our hour of need,
In those moments of confusing choices,
In the nights before medical surgery,
In the room of farewell to a loved one.
We lean on the heart of your compassion
Assured that we will not be left alone.

Today: The *Vigilant One* is with me.

Teacher

John 3:2

I imagine myself among those you taught
On the hillsides, eager for your message.
I hear you speak of the kind of deeds
You hope we'll do in our stingy world,
Of the requirement to love our enemy
And to really forgive those who hurt us.
I hear you tell of treating our neighbor
The way we ourselves want to be treated.
And then I imagine we all get up and leave,
Return home, and truly change our hearts.

Today: I focus on living one of the *Teacher's* messages.

Sailor on the Sea of Life

From a distance the ride looks inviting,
Smoothly gliding along with full speed,
But when I get inside the boat with you
I notice that sailing is much like my life.
Going *with* the wind is the easy part
While a definite expertise is required
To turn and sail *into* a hearty wind,
To move the rudder, to tack the sails
With a zig and a zag, trying to stay upright.
When I sail with you I'd better be alert.

Today: I remain alert to how the *Sailor* guides me.

All-Powerful One

How potent your emanating energy.
Swift enough to shape wild rivers
And bend the way their waters run.
Strong enough to lessen violence,
Yet war, hatred, and conflict persist.
What can we expect from your power?
An influence of love, not domination,
Sweeping through the human heart.
A force of perpetual kindness, not fear,
Drawing us with magnetic affection.

Today: The *All-Powerful One* moves me toward peace.

Binder of Wounds

Psalm 147:3

Deep and cavernous are the inner gashes
Of those rejected, abused, abandoned.
You bind the shreds of injured self-worth
With your tender touch of solicitude,
Stitch together the wounded spirit
With the meticulous skill of a surgeon.
Some wounds take a long time to heal
And require a huge amount of patience.
You never cease tending to our hurts
And waiting with us as they slowly mend.

Today: I unite with the world's wounded ones.

My Rock

Isaiah 26:1–4

When that which was once rewarding
Is trampled under the belly of disaster,
When the train of hope leaves the station
And I have not yet purchased a ticket,
When the ground of my faith dissolves
And I feel there is nothing worthwhile,
Your firm base rests under my fissures.
Amid the crumbling of my pretensions
Your constancy and unbreakable solidity
Offer assurance in spite of my losses.

Today: I stand my hope on the *Rock*.

Brightness of Souls

Davelyn Vignaud

Each soul is suffused with your flowing grace
Of luminosity, a beam of brilliance so intense
That everything veiled would be aglow
If the body were shed. A radiance stronger
Than sun, softer than moon, steady as silence,
Spreads outward from every soul that exists.
Together they spin into your great Light
Until you penetrate each particle of darkness.
Oh, that we could see all of creation as a swath
Of brilliant soul-shining, illuminating love!

Today: I merge my love with the *Brightness of Souls*.

Holy Midwife

Barbara Marian

Every day a little birthing awaits us,
An opportunity pregnant with possibility.
Some of these spiritual birthings go easy.
Others are long, difficult, and agonizing.
You, Holy Midwife, attend each delivery
And urge us toward expectant growth.
Remind us that we must to do our part.
Breathe in. Breathe out. Let go. Let go.
Trust the painful contractions of labor
Preceding the precious life that follows.

Today: I listen to *Holy Midwife* urging my growth.

Counselor

Psalm 16:7

I come to you for guidance
And you nod silently.
I tell you stories of pain
And you cry in response.
I offer my heart's secrets
And you seem not to hear.
What kind of counselor are you?
Where are the answers I seek?
Are they to be found
In ways I cannot yet imagine?

Today: I am patient as I await counsel.

Companion of the Lonely

You hold the hand of lonely ones
As they walk in their dark valleys
Of empty isolation and strayed love.
The widowed, the childless, the lost,
Aged ones never visited, the rejected,
The dying with no one by their side,
Refugees in camps, disabled veterans,
Children abandoned by their parents,
And all those who have not been loved.
We can be your companionship for them.

Today: I reach out to someone lonely.

Keeper of Souls

Keep the song in my soul,
Let it not lose its music.
Keep the holy in my soul,
Let it not ignore its source.
Keep the love in my soul,
Let it not close in on self.
Keep the light in my soul,
Let it not forget to shine.
Keep the vision in my soul,
Let it not lose sight of you.

Today: I remember the *Keeper* of my soul.

---✝️---

Seeker of Hearts

Hearts wild and free.
Hearts tame and serene.
Hearts open and true.
Hearts closed and false.
Hearts full and heavy.
Hearts empty and lean.
You seek them all
And ask for one thing only:
That each be the bearer
Of your unconditional love.

Today: I let my heart be found.

Stronghold for the Oppressed

Psalm 9:9

In remote cells of political prisoners,
In huts and shacks of poverty's people,
In all places where there is tyranny,
You provide the strength of endurance.
You bring them no weapon but love,
No armor except that of compassion.
Requesting that those of us with plenty
Bring our love, our prayer, our action
So their afflictions may be diminished
And life's bleakness be less intense.

Today: I do my part to lessen injustice of any kind.

---+---

Source of Knowledge

No informational source can tell me
Where my soul originated
Or solve the mystery
Of why some live and some die.
No matter how much I search
For certain knowledge
Only you hold the treasure
To life's deepest questions,
Only you know the vast secrets
Behind the curtain of life.

Today: I humbly accept how little I know.

Peace Bringer

John 20:19–20

Not all wars consist of armored soldiers.
Many take place within feuding individuals
Where jealousy, anger, and hatred exist.
Peace Bringer, come to all hearts at war.
Move them to lay down their weapons,
To cast aside bitterness and resentment.
Bring your peace to hardhearted ones.
Lessen the grip of those who desire revenge.
May your peace release whatever binds
And free all those held captive by hostility.

Today: I let go of any feuding that exists in my heart.

Fountain of Wisdom

When the mind loses its ability to think clearly
And the heart is unable to follow its true direction,
When the spirit gasps for even a teaspoon of truth
And the body is clogged with the sand of exhaustion,
There arises from within your fullness of grace
An oasis of relief like welcome desert streams.
Weighty choices and difficult decisions begin to shift
As the flow of your sacred guidance clears the space.
That which was clouded, clogged, and exhausted
Washes away in the clear water of your wisdom.

Today: The *Fountain of Wisdom* flows within me.

NOVEMBER 18

---✝---

Upright Judge

Hebrews 12:23

I come before you, Upright Judge,
Trusting in the fairness of your approach,
Sure that your opinions are based on love.
On what grounds do you bring me to court?
For what thoughts, words, and deeds
Do you now hold me accountable?
Could it be my ever-troubling selfishness
Or the unfair criticisms in my mind and mouth?
You have every right to search my heart.
I, too, desire my love to expand beyond myself.

Today: I have confidence in the *Upright Judge*.

My Center

When undulating activities tilt our days
And threaten to throw us off balance,
When prayer strains under pressures
Of not-enough-time and nothing-happens,
When those we care about are pained
And we nearly cave in from our caring,
You continue to be a hub of stillness,
A nucleus of love, our core equilibrium.
No matter how out of control we spin,
You remain the peaceful Center for us.

Today: *My Center* keeps me balanced.

She Who Hears the Cries of the World

Chinese

Like Asian portrayals of Kuan Yin
As an enlightened being of compassion,
So is your ear pressed toward creation,
Listening intently for the least cry of distress,
Searching for every living being that suffers,
Weeping with those whose tears abound,
Sorrowing for those desolate and bereft,
Moaning with those whose hurt is unending.
Bend your ear nearer. Come close. Come close.
For many corners of life cry out with pain.

Today: I bend my ear toward those who hurt.

God of All Generations

From endless ages, in the most ancient of times
Your unique DNA of love spiraled into existence,
Giving humanity's heart the gene of your presence.
You stirred our ancestors toward their best
Even though they sometimes lived their worst.
With every human birthing came a fresh possibility
To activate the purest form of loving kindness.
Will our spiritual DNA survive and thrive?
Will we be a strong connection for living our best
So your love can pass on to the next generation?

Today: My spiritual DNA is activated.

---+---

Faithful Love

Psalm 136

Have I ever known you to truly fail me?
Has there been a time when you let me down?
Have I come to you and not been heard?
Your silence has led me to doubt and question
When I lost my sense of you, time and again.
Upsetting events and circumstances distanced us.
Eventually, I heard you whisper in the darkness.
Only in looking back did I see how you held me,
Continually courted me with your kindheartedness.
Gradually I became assured of your unending fidelity.

Today: *Faithful Love* reassures my trust.

Tree of Life

All of us, small and large, old and young,
From every color, creed, and country,
Whether we dress in poor rags or fine riches
We are branches of your one eternal life.
Intimately united, unmistakably connected
In both origin, diversity, and destination,
A multitude of species with a sacred union.
How can antagonism and hatred be possible?
Why does anyone try to break the branches?
What causes humanity to deny this oneness?

Today: I respect all branches on the *Tree of Life*.

Precious Pearl

Matthew 13:45–46

Do I search for you as passionately
As the merchant sought for his pearl?
Do I value my inner life as fully
As he assessed his precious discovery?
What would it take for me to "sell all"
So I could give you more of my heart?
How can I be focused like that merchant
And have you become my center?
Which of my negative habits must cease
So our love relationship can grow?

Today: I assess what I value most.

NOVEMBER 25

All Beneficent

The Qur'an

When I reflect upon the benefits
Of my being in relationship with you
A basketful of responses tumbles forth
And lays its overflowing gifts at my doorstep.
They include fullness for my emptiness,
Emptiness for my over-abundance,
Deep peace for my inner discordance,
Inner discordance for my easy apathy.
I now perceive how each piece of life
Includes the touch of your beneficence.

Today: I ponder the *All Beneficent* in my life.

---†---

The Satisfier

Psalm 107:8–9

How ironic that those who have plenty
Worry excessively about possible shortage,
While those who live with scarceness
Voice gratitude for the little they have.
The illusion of scarcity in abundance,
The appreciation of those with much less,
Which of these trusts your generosity?
Whose heart leans on yours as Provider:
The one stressed and exceedingly anxious
Or the one applauding simple abundance?

Today: I am grateful for what I have.

The Restorer of Balance

Philippians 4:13

When the limbs of our loyalty weaken
And the desire to stand upright falters,
When the lamp of love grows dark
And faith lessens with anxious illusion,
When the ability to go forward in joy
Teeters awkwardly on broken dreams,
We turn to you, our Restorer of Balance.
We accept your inherent stability in us
And begin our spiritual practice again,
Slowly building up what has declined.

Today: My spiritual practice renews me.

The Place

Jewish

*M*akom is how some refer to you
In the rabbinic tradition of word-play.
Awesome encounters in biblical travel
Arise in surprising locations where you,
The Place, reveal another aspect of yourself.
Burning bushes, dreams of ladders,
Angels sent as urgent messengers,
Clouds that pilot wanderers on the way.
All these lead to sacred places where you
Manifest as "the Place" of great holiness.

Today: The place where I am is where *The Place* is.

The First and the Last

Revelation 1:8

Alpha and Omega, two simple Greek words
Found on many church altars and art,
Reminders for those who see and perceive
That you are the bookends of existence.
You are the hidden architect of all that is,
There before the world we know was born,
There when the unknown future will end.
The momentum of life and death is yours
For you view, as none of us can,
The journey each one takes and its fulfillment.

Today: I am at peace between the bookends.

┼

Companion

Luke 24:13–35

Companion: *cum panis*, Latin for "with bread."
Scriptural memories of how you were present
At the farewell table, blessing, breaking, sharing.
Being on the road with discouraged disciples,
Revelation coming forth, again blessing bread.
Today, your companioning still brings bread
To each who meets you at table or on the road.
The bread of kinship and hope. The inner peace
That the heart requires and each person desires,
The nourishing sustenance to keep love alive.

Today: I encounter the *Companion*.

December

God's complexity is daunting: God is probably not a person, place, gender, consciousness, time, or anything else I can conceive. We humans will never understand the full nature of an infinitely omnipotent God. Yet I have grown to cherish the mystery. And I have been blessed for decades with nonstop gifts from this loving source of goodness. That is why I know with certitude that God is the grandest gift of all. Faith is my humble expression of gratitude.

—*Barbara J. Kouba*

Quiet One

Into the din of our inner confusion
You come, gentle as a single snowflake.
Into the rush of our continual hurry
You come, slow as a melting icicle.
Into the pressure of endless activity
You come, easy as restful breathing.
Into the constant voices of demand
You come, silent as a falling star.
Quiet One, restorer of stillness,
You are present. Waiting to be welcomed.

Today: I stop long enough to welcome the *Quiet One*.

Spirit of Joy

Zephaniah 3:17

Come, Spirit of Joy, come!
Be reborn in us. Birth enthusiasm.
Leap into our minds with gladness.
Dance away dismal discouragement.
Toss out griping and antipathies.
Topple old fortifications of blame.
Chase away what creates sadness.
Loosen all that keeps out your joy.
Hasten our footsteps to happiness.
Fulfill the designs of your heart.

Today: My spirit leaps with renewed joy.

DECEMBER 3

✝

Messiah

Matthew 1:1

The promised one, anticipated savior,
Sought after to ease the world's pain.
The one thought to surely bring peace.
The people waited. Finally you came
With the gift of teaching and healing.
Your life revealed a generous divinity,
Bequeathed the world a legacy of love.
Has your coming made a difference?
Have your teachings changed the world?
Has your love influenced my heart?

Today: The *Messiah*'s coming influences my life.

Lord

"Lord." That word sounds extremely patriarchal.
Definite. No compromising. Heavy-handed.
"Lording it over," so the phrase goes,
Implying one who wields power callously.
But your coming to dwell among us
Expressed the very opposite of this.
You, Lord, washed feet, touched lepers,
Wept with the grieving, forgave sinners.
You did not over-power. You *empowered*.
Restoring dignity and self-confidence.

Today: I recognize how the *Lord* empowers me.

Dayspring from on High

Luke 1:78

You are the bright sunrise after obscure night,
The breaking of light after a bleak horizon.
You are the spreading dawn of something new,
The vivid splendor on the horizon of hope.
You originate from an eternal source of kindness
Hidden in the deep fissures of ancient mystery.
You rise more resplendent than the blazing sun,
Showing forth light to all who wait in darkness.
You assure us we are able to find your peace
If we but turn ourselves around toward you.

Today: I turn myself toward the *Dayspring*.

Great Whisper
That Calms

Mark Nepo

Whisper in my distracted ear
When all I can hear is the whine
Of my crammed calendar.
Whisper in my worried heart
When a loved one's pain falls
Into every crevice of my life.
Whisper in my addled mind
When I lose my way to love
By constant, heartless criticism.
Whisper loud enough for me to hear.

Today: I listen closely to the *Great Whisper*.

The Cosmic Christ

Pierre Teilhard de Chardin

Spirit and matter echo each other in jubilation.
Your resurrected presence encircles all that exists.
Love is strewn throughout the beautiful Cosmos,
Gathering the elements into a holy embrace,
Dancing among ancient and newly birthed stars,
Resting among silent stones of glacial heritage,
Alive with graced movement in the human heart,
Splendid reverberation, replete with mystery.
Your presence, beyond the confines of rationality,
Bears intimacy enough to entwine us into one.

Today: I am one with *The Cosmic Christ*.

DECEMBER 8

Promised One

Reaching through the ages with compassion,
A pledge to send humankind a beloved.
This One would enter the entangled fray
And touch hearts anxious for a welcome,
Heal brokenness and forgive the worst sin.
Then you came forth as this Promised One,
Entered life's harsh arena and heralded hope,
Brought love beyond anyone's expectation
And offered sacred teachings to last a lifetime.
Why, then, are our hearts still yearning?

Today: I welcome the *Promised One*.

$+$

Sacred Darkness

When the desire to go forward lessens,
When the brightness of insight dims,
When the hope of finding a way fails,
It is then that I enter into your darkness
And find a nest in your sheltering womb.
Entering the hushed cave of your heart
I abide in the shadow of your presence,
Turning toward that which is not seen
But known in faith, accepted with hope.
Resting there, I am enveloped in your love.

Today: I find a secure nest in *Sacred Darkness*.

┼

Prince of Peace

Isaiah 9:6

Peace. The seed of it in every heart, every nation.
The possibility of a life and a world of nonviolence.
Prince. Ruler. Desiring harmony for one and all.
But peace cannot be forced onto anyone,
Not even by you who reign with ultimate authority.
Peace evolves as individual minds and hearts change,
Willing to lay aside what causes dissension,
Open to discuss differences and divisive difficulties,
Ready to listen generously to another point of view.
Prince of Peace, may you reign in our hearts.

Today: The *Prince of Peace* rules my heart.

Wonderful Counselor

Isaiah 9:6

What if I were able to sit across from you
And listen closely to your counsel for me?
To what deepening course would you point?
Is there a certain guidance you would give
To draw me nearer to you in my living?
Is there some pertinent question you would ask
To give clarity to my closeted vision?
What if I began today to really listen to you?
What if I heard within our meeting space
The wise advice that could change my heart?

Today: I listen to the counsel being offered to me.

DECEMBER 12

---†---

Dwelling Place

Exodus 25:8

You, my Dwelling Place,
Have created my inner self
Into a sanctuary of love.
I carry splendor and goodness
With every step,
With every breath,
With every word,
With every act.
What an honor it is
To contain you, the Holy One.

Today: I remember my *Dwelling Place*.

The Word

John 1:1–5

Words, words, words, and more words,
Spoken, written, throughout history and life.
None can compare with you, the Word,
A message complete and all-encompassing,
Sent forth to humanity from the Great Heart
To speak the completeness of all words: Love.
O Word of the Holy, your message is alive,
Written in covenantal script never to be erased.
May each common word coming forth from me
Echo the magnificent love of you, the one Word.

Today: *The Word* is reflected in my words.

Most High

Psalm 91:9

Transcendent, outwardly far away,
Yet, you stretch forth to touch us
With a Child born of motherly flesh.
You enter our world small in size,
Vulnerable as a newly birthed one.
You are Most High, but also Most Near,
So close that we feel your loving breath
In each detail and circumstance of life,
Bridging illusive, vast space between us
With the blessedness of your humanity.

Today: The *Most High* is close to me.

Desired of All Nations

Haggai 2:8

Oh, that you were sought after and desired
By every nation, large or small, strong or weak.
Underneath dominance, greed, and differences,
Leaders of nations and their country's inhabitants
Long for that which is available from your heart:
Peace, respect, freedom, equality, and prosperity.
All these you gladly give to those open to receive.
Desired of All Nations, how is it we stray so far?
Return us, each and all, to that basic human desire,
To be at peace with you, ourselves, and others.

Today: I do my part to engender peace.

The Gift

Christmas presents. Gifts bestowed
And received. Maybe a surprise or two.
You, the Gift surpassing all other gifts,
Bring us more than we might expect.
Presents that did not make our list,
Something to wear on the inside of us
Such as truth, generosity, patience,
Reconciliation, and respect for one another.
Each Christmas, another gift of growth.
What will you gift us with this year?

Today: I think about what my heart needs.

✝

Wisdom from the Most High

Breviary, O Antiphons

O Wisdom from the Most High,
Bring to us now your perceptive guidance.
Clear out our noise so we hear your voice.
Help us calm our frenetic hearts and minds.
Persuade us to open ourselves to you.
Enter our resistances and determinations.
Influence what lies unresolved on our path.
Counsel us when we forget you are near.
Steer us again and again toward the path
That leads us to integrity and truth.

Today: I follow the counsel of Holy *Wisdom*.

DECEMBER 18

Ruler of the
House of Israel

Breviary, O Antiphons

Bring your rule over the house of my heart
As you did long ago with the tribe of Israel.
I will clear my inner room of its egoism
Until I have sufficient space to welcome you.
I will open the window and freshen the air
So I can carry the fragrance of your goodness.
I will light the fireplace and kindle my spirit
Until it flames high with enthusiasm for you.
I will stand by the door and wait expectantly
For you to come and fill my house with love.

Today: I prepare my inner house.

Flower of Jesse's Stem

Breviary, O Antiphons

From the old roots of an ancient lineage
A lengthy gestation of ancestry ensues.
Hidden in the flow of common life
A green stem rises, full of promise.
Personages filled with light and shadow
Nourish the stem, feed the budding growth.
Ages pass. Finally the bud of hope opens
And the longed for Promised One appears.
A flower in the shape of human form
With blossoms the color of divinity.

Today: I reflect on my spiritual ancestry.

Key of David

Breviary, O Antiphons

Little Mary of *The Secret Garden* seeks the key
To the long-locked gate of what lies inside.
With persistence, she hunts to find the way,
Deliberately setting out, searching, seeking.
The buried key is discovered. The gate opens.
The neglected garden's beauty is restored.
In faith I set out to find you, the secreted key
Opening my heart-gate and freeing love within,
Leading to the garden where virtue blooms.
You are that Key. Come, open what has closed in me.

Today: I look for the *Key*.

Radiant Dawn

Breviary, O Antiphons

Divine Brightness on the heart's horizon,
Light slowly breaking through the long night,
Your bright presence dawns anew each day,
Ever awakening what has grown sleepy in us.
Your tapestry of light sparkles in the heart,
Coloring each portion of the day with hope.
Arise in those gloomy places of our discontent.
Shine through the gray shadows of night.
Spread your robust beams of encouragement
Through the thick layers of our unhappiness.

Today: The gloom in me is overcome by hope.

King of the Nations

Breviary, O Antiphons

Would that it were true, your authority
Over the nations could cease endless war.
Would that it were true, your reign
Of love in hearts could end entitlement.
Would that it were true, your supremacy
Of the mind could halt ego pursuits.
King of the Nations, Ruler of Hearts,
When will each of us turn toward you
And reflect your compassionate leadership?
When will your kingship rule my own heart?

Today: I pray for rulers of nations and for myself.

✝

Emmanuel

Breviary, O Antiphons

You have come near, God-with-us.
Not only made your home among us,
You have come to dwell within us
Making of our heart a habitat of divinity.
At each moment of every single day
You open the way for us to love,
To go beyond our selfish inclinations,
To seek the good in each person,
To eliminate the barriers that divide,
To be a welcoming home worthy of you.

Today: I am a habitat of love.

Child of Bethlehem

So easy to place you on a spotless pedestal,
Forgetting how you came to dwell with us,
Came, as all children come into this world,
A small babe with a bloody umbilical cord,
A wee infant nuzzling your mother's breast,
Crying out in need and filling your diapers.
How tremendous the truth of your incarnation,
Humbling yourself to vulnerable dependency.
O Child of Bethlehem, for every child alive today
Protect them in their poverty of defenselessness.

Today: I join my heart with the children of the world.

Incarnate One

Over these two thousand and more years
Have we become immune to your embodiment?
Has the reality of your fleshy humanness
Become a mere glazed remembrance of joy?
Perhaps this Christmas the surprise will re-awaken.
We will be open-mouthed in awe at your coming.
Our wonder will surpass what consumes our lives.
We will look with fresh awareness at who you are,
Learning from you, rededicated to live your teachings
Until our fleshiness, too, radiates genuine love.

Today: The *Incarnate One's* coming amazes me.

Son of Mary

That first look into your mother's eyes,
The love you beheld looking back at you.
Were you both enthralled with each other?
Her young arms that cradled you safely
Would embrace you again at your death,
But this painful part of your life was hidden
As you rested in her complete attention.
Son of Mary, child of a pure-hearted mother,
You are with me from birth through death,
Holding me the way your mother held you.

Today: The *Son of Mary* beholds me with love.

Hope for the World

Amid a warring world desperate for global peace
You enter as our Songbird, our Encouragement,
Hope for those whose optimism is exceedingly thin.
You are that little bird perching on the soul's branch,
The one that poet Emily Dickinson introduced.
The feathered creature singing an endless melody
Carried to every heart gone silent from dejection.
Your determined song of hope insists we not give up.
Faltering humanity can reach toward one another
And restore a heartfelt belief in our original goodness.

Today: I renew my hope.

Comforter

O Comforter, you provide the covering
Of warmth, a soft quilt of gentleness
To guard against the chilly gusts of pain,
A kindly wrap to keep impending rigidity
From taking over the frosty, wintered heart.
For when the cold, harsh setbacks of life
Rush in with strong, congealing forcefulness
They can easily numb the hurting heart.
Your presence keeps our hesitant love flowing
In spite of the insistent coldness filling us.

Today: I comfort someone whose heart seems cold.

+

Lord of Hosts

Isaiah 2:12

How could there not be a great host of those
Who seek you as the focus of their hearts?
Multitudes of ordinary people place you
As the first and most central in their lives.
Many do so quietly, without any fanfare.
No white robes like those in the scriptures.
No showy behavior or spectacular speeches.
Their lives show their intentional commitment,
Evidence of their faithfulness, true to you.
What will it take for me to join this multitude?

Today: My life reveals my heart's focus.

DECEMBER 30

The One Who
Is Always Now

J. Philip Newell

Not even a heartbeat away from me,
You, the One who is always now, always here.
It is I who stray in thought, word, and deed.
It is I who miss the miracle of the moment.
It is I whose rhythm disregards the heartbeat
Of your steady, reassuring presence.
Each day, to renew mindfulness of you,
Each night, to deliberately turn toward you,
To you, the One Who Is Always Now,
Whose love forever beckons me to be attentive.

Today: I am attuned to the *One Who Is Always Now.*

✝

Gate-Keeper

Wisdom 6:14

Divine Gate-Keeper, ever present to my soul,
I approach the open gate of the new year
Aware of my vulnerability and mortality,
Recognizing my dependence on your vigilance.
Your wisdom will direct my inner footsteps
As I face the future's unmarked terrain.
Your rapt attentiveness assures me
That you will guide my comings and goings.
This day I join my heart with all living beings
As we walk together toward what lies ahead.

Today: I walk with hope into the new year.

My
Beloved said,
"My name is not complete without yours."
I thought:
How could a human's worth ever be such?
And God knowing all our thoughts—and all our
thoughts are innocent steps on the path—
then addressed my heart,
God revealed
a sublime truth to the world,
when (God) sang,
"I am made whole by your life. Each soul,
each soul completes me."

—Hafiz

REFERENCES

Epigraph

Rilke's Book of Hours: Love Poems to God, translated by Anita Barrows and Joanna Macy. New York: Riverhead Books, 1996. *"Ich Lese es heraus aus deinem Wort,"* 55.

Introduction

Rilke's Book of Hours: Love Poems to God, translated by Anita Barrows and Joanna Macy. New York: Riverhead Books, 1996. *"Du bist die Zukunft, grofses Morgenrot,"* p. 119; *"Wir dürfen dick nicht eigenmächtig malen,"* 50.

January

Cohen, Leonard. *Book of Mercy.* Toronto: McClelland and Stewart Limited, 1984, 47.

February

Kushner, Lawrence. *Eyes Remade for Wonder.* Woodstock, Vermont: Jewish Lights Publishing, 1998, 144.

March

Taylor, Barbara Brown. *God in Pain: Sermons on Suffering.* Nashville, Tennessee: Abingdon Press, 1998, 20.

April

Muller, Wayne. *Learning to Pray: How We Find Heaven on Earth.* New York: Bantam Books, 2003, 44–45.

May

Gateley, Edwina. *A Mystical Heart: 52 Weeks in the Presence of God.* New York: Crossroad, 1998, 98.

June

Johnson, Elizabeth A. *She Who Is: The Mystery of God in Feminist Theological Discourse.* New York: Crossroad, 1993, 117–118.

July

McLeod, Melvin. "What's Right With Islam: Interview with Imam Feisal Abdul Rauf." *Shambhala Sun* (July 2004), 54.

August

Prevallet, Elaine M. *Making the Shift: Seeing Faith through a New Lens.* Nerinx, Kentucky: Sisters of Loretto, 2006, 41–42.

September

Prabhavananda, Swami. *Sermon on the Mount According to Vedanta.* Hollywood, California: Vedanta Society of Southern California, 1992, 78.

October

Rahner, Karl. *Karl Rahner: Spiritual Writings.* Edited with an Introduction by Philip Endean. Maryknoll, New York: Orbis Books, 2004, 80.

November

Chittister, Joan. *In Search of Belief*. Liguori, Missouri: Liguori Publications, 1999, 23.

December

Kouba, Barbara J. "I Love You For Hating Me: A Struggling Believer Encounters the Divine." *America* (August 17–24, 2009), 26–28.

Postscript

Ladinsky, Daniel. *Love Poems from God: Twelve Sacred Voices from the East and West*. New York: Penguin Putnam, 2002, 179.

DIVINE NAMES INDEX

SCRIPTURE INDEX